EARLY PRAISE FOR *Travels in Vermeer*

"A memoir exploring how Johannes Vermeer's paintings bestow bountiful gifts. . . . White's descriptions are sensuous, precise, and evocative. . . . [He] praises Vermeer for his sensitivity to 'anatomies of intimate, unguarded moments,' a sensitivity that White himself brings to his luminous readings of the paintings. An enchanting book about the transformative power of art." —*KIRKUS REVIEWS*

"All the sorrow of love is compressed into Michael White's memoir. So, too, is all the consolation of art. Nothing I've read translates so closely the expectant hush of Vermeer's paintings into language or suggests so eloquently what they hold for a contemporary viewer, not a specialist but an ordinary grieving soul who might travel a quarter way around the world to look at them. Figures it took a poet to get it this beautifully, thrillingly right." —PETER TRACHTENBERG

"What happens to a soul in conflict with its life in the world? In these pages, it travels deeply into art, into the complex and beautiful answers there. This book is a treasure and a guide. It is a type of healing for the intellect and the heart." —REBECCA LEE

"This memoir will enable you to relish first-hand a wide sea of art—the painting, the painter; the poem, the poet—while you experience the deep drama of the author's life. A unique dance among genres, this memoir's clear and powerful descriptions touch on the mysteries of seduction, loss, and the artistic impulse ' _____ how time *can* be interrupted." 'GERTON

ALSO BY MICHAEL WHITE

Vermeer in Hell (2014)
Re-entry (2006)
Palma Cathedral (1998)
The Island (1993)

Travels in Vermeer | A MEMOIR

Michael White

A Karen & Michael Braziller Book

PERSEA BOOKS | NEW YORK

The author wishes to thank the editors of the following periodicals in which pieces from *Travels in Vermeer* have appeared, sometimes in slightly different versions: *The Journal* ("Prelude" and "Amsterdam"), *The Florida Review* ("View of Delft"), and *Image: Art, Faith, Mystery* ("Woman Holding a Balance").

Lines quoted by Elizabeth Bishop are from "The Moose" in *The Complete Poems 1927–1979* by Elizabeth Bishop (Farrar, Straus & Giroux, 1983). Used by permission of the publisher.

Lines quoted by Donald Justice are from "Men at Forty," in *Collected Poems* by Donald Justice, copyright © 2004 by Donald Justice. Used by permission of Alfred A Knopf, an imprint of the Knopf Doubleday Publishing Group, a division of Random House LLC. All rights reserved.

Persea Books, Inc.
277 Broadway
New York, New York 10007

Library of Congress Cataloging-in-Publication Data
White, Michael, 1956–
Travels in Vermeer : a memoir / Michael White.
      pages cm
"A Karen and Michael Braziller Book."
ISBN 978-0-89255-437-9 (alk. paper)
1. White, Michael, 1956–2. Vermeer, Johannes, 1632–1675—Miscellanea. I. Title.
PS3573.H47445Z46 2015
811'.54–dc23
[B]
          014016180

Design and composition by Rita Lascaro. Set in Minion.
Manufactured in the United States of America
First Edition

CONTENTS

TRAVELS IN VERMEER

She strikes you stock-still from a distance, though you don't know how or why. For she isn't pretty exactly, this woman busy at her work, her face downturned but angled into the light that rakes across the scene from left to right. She might be a lace-maker, or a lady of means. She might be a kitchen maid, who pours milk from an earthenware pitcher as lightly, as expertly, as if she were cradling a baby. It's always the same room, but a different fantasy. Here she stands, at the still point of another world.

PRELUDE

[*October*]

There's a small window cut into my front door, composed of four identical square panes with a perfect cross of slim, oak muntins dividing them. Sometimes I stand at the door, staring idly at a neighbor walking his dog outside or at the rain drizzling through the longleaf branches—slicking down my front sidewalk—or at nothing. I rest my forehead on the juncture of this cross. It dents the skin of my forehead, and is oddly comforting.

It's already October, 2003, the grass a matte gray. The house is silent, except for the chronic ringing in my ears. If I were standing on the beach five miles away, I might notice how the glass-green rollers, folding over the offshore sandbars, have turned slate-gray. I might notice how the currents, plying the lap of sand, have switched from south to north and the surfers have donned their wetsuits. But I haven't been to the beach for months. Here, in downtown Wilmington, North Carolina, the pines are releasing their summer needles: drifts of blonde straw are piling up on the slopes of my roof and snuffing out what little life remains in the lawn.

I'm in the midst of a bad divorce, and have nearly lost what's left of my wits trekking from lawyer's office to courtroom to mediation to counseling and through all the blank space in-between. Nearly all the anxiety on my end has to do with my daughter, Sophia, who is only three. Sara—my beautiful, considerably younger, estranged wife—has a shark of a lawyer and is seeking full custody.

Turns out I'm not quite the man I thought I was. The one who dealt with his alcoholism half a lifetime ago and still keeps up a contented and continuous sobriety. The devoted husband who stood beside his first wife through her battle with cancer; who did all he could to help her pass with courage and dignity. The poet who earned his doctorate, published books, stubbornly found his share of success. The passionate, popular, outdoorsy, "cool" professor. I'm not sure where that guy, *any* of those guys, went. At home, there are convulsive fits of sobbing, once or twice a day, and I am taken aback by how long this lasts. At the university where I teach, a lingering sensation of falling dogs me in the halls. Friends have taken sides. Department meetings are dreadful. But I still manage to pump myself up for classes. I still gladly lose myself in the earnest faces of students, trying to inspire them.

Now it's Saturday, two weeks after the temporary custody hearing. It's only the first step in what, in North Carolina, is a yearlong process, but so far nothing seems to be going my way. I'd wanted a fifty/fifty custody split; what I got is the traditional every-other-weekend visitation. I'm sitting in my armchair, in a colorless, dreamless haze of therapist-recommended Lexapro, staring at my own feet, when a loud knock jolts me out of my skin. I rise, furtively, in order to steal a glance through the door without being seen. It's Sara: a whiff of beauty in the frame. I think: *No.* Another curveball. Because my divorce is crazy and bitter and acrimonious, and because the stakes (my relationship with my daughter) are high, there's safety in distance, in a locked door. I sit back down. But, a moment later, she knocks again—a cordial but slightly impatient rap. I start to get up, then sit back down, and cross my arms.

Suddenly, I realize the door isn't locked so, staying low, I make it the three steps to the doorknob in the same instant it begins to turn. I'm fumbling with the chain too late as she pushes the door open about a foot until it stops against my right knee. Then I peer through the little square window.

Sometimes, time speeds up: not just an hour, but months flash past. Other times, it stops—the weight of everything, past present future bearing down. One thing I know: in the time it takes to open one's mouth, to reach for the dangling chainlock, what happened or would happen in court in the minds of others doesn't count, what happens now is what counts.

Here's what I see. Sara in a black raincoat, hair cut in a sharply angled pageboy—dyed a richer shade of black, her huge brown eyes outlined dramatically, her lips a flame-red jolt against the gray world. She's holding a fresh-baked vanilla custard pie in each hand. When she catches my eye, she raises one pie up next to her ear, so I can see it clearly: *See*? Then she nods for me to let her in.

I realize that the language of this encounter—pies and lipstick, raincoat absurdly open on the lightly freckled swell of her breasts— might seem like some sort of joke. Maybe it's even outrageous, a cliché, for this to happen weeks after she left me amid a flurry of scandalous accusations. But it's dead serious for me.

I'd always done most of the cooking, but one thing Sara had done for five years in the kitchen is ply me with desserts. I didn't really have a sweet tooth at first, so it was sport for her. She spent years whipping up crunchy Christmas toffees, gooey brownies, frothy coconut macaroons for me, but when it turned out that I couldn't be trusted alone in the same room with a simple vanilla custard pie—for there'd be nothing left but a few crumbs on the counter—*that* was a triumph.

As for the raincoat. Our relationship might be dysfunctional, absurd, and riddled with clichés, it might swallow its pride and show up with a pie in each hand, but when we made love, we made love, and we did it body and soul. We'd rowed across long summers, years of darkness—headboard battering potholes into the plaster wall behind it, sheets drenched in the Carolina mugginess which she had loved to let in—years of love that cannot be unmade. Such a fleeting dream of eternity: seen only in glimpses, flights beyond ourselves until we fell gasping into each other's arms.

Then she starts to push open the door. "Sara?" I say, puzzled, as she puts her weight into it hard. I'm bracing my hip to meet her. "Wait," I say, though of course I don't mean *wait*, I mean *stop*. She manages to jam her shoe through the door, then most of her leg, so I relent a little: I don't want to hurt her. I hold all my weight on the door, and I know she can't budge it, but I try not to push back any more than necessary—not an easy thing to do. She shoves back hard a couple of times anyway—my mind spinning a zillion miles an hour, trying to take it in, react correctly—this beautiful, panicky girl in trench coat, bearing her considerable gifts on a blasé, brown-grass day, one long leg muscling through her former front door, with a golden, cellophane-covered, still-warm pie in each hand. We're locked for a good half-minute in this pantomime. I can smell the cinnamon mixed with Sara's own orchidaceous scent. Then she gives up, pulls back her leg through the door our former friends once entered without knocking, and I slam it and set the chain to be sure.

For a few seconds, through the window, we read each other's eyes. Despite everything, all the manipulations of our divorce, the somewhat irrelevant boyfriend (who'd hang up when I happened to answer), what anyone dignified or rational would think about the attempt she is making, I truly feel for her. I wish I could let her in. I *want* to let her in; in another moment, I think, I will do it. I'll ask her to sit down, brew coffee, and cut pie for us both. I'll ask what's on her mind.

I lean my forehead against the cross. Today, in this dreary light, Sara is irresistibly lovely. I remember the day our daughter, Sophia, was born. When the nurse announced, "It's a girl," I danced—unself-consciously, for once—around the room in the flapping hospital gown. In the moments after, the nurse preparing to clean her up, Sophia lay quietly on the table. Not a peep. Then, cautiously, her tongue snaked straight up out of her mouth, and made two or three tentative circles in the air. Testing, tasting the atmosphere. Sara was exhausted, her eyes unfocused beneath dank bangs. Within the half hour, by prior agreement, I went out for two-dozen gooey-hot Krispy Kreme doughnuts, which we gobbled up with cold white milk before the new mom slept for twelve straight hours.

Of course, I think, she's broken up with the new boyfriend, so she's here to reclaim the life she'd so recently vacated, as if nothing much had happened. *What is your problem?* she seems to convey with a childishly scrunched pout: *Just open the damn door!*

I don't show it, I keep my expression deadpan, but I'm torn with hope, with hurt. If she says, *I'm sorry*, I decide, I'll open the door. I will. I watch intently, waiting. *Say it.*

For years I'll imagine this moment, dream of it, maybe for the rest of my life.

She bends down at the foot of the door, the squeaking storm door still propped open by her hip. Then she rises, steps free, looks me dead in the eye again, and turns. I watch as she strides across the grass to the grayish Accord that was once ours, gets in, drives off. I keep looking, my thoughts racing: *What just happened? What did I do?*

I stand for a long time, forehead pressed against the cross in the window. Then I open the front door. Holding the storm door open a few inches is one of the pies. The other pie is out on the porch next to some disused flowerpots. I lean down and pick up the pie at my feet—still warm and fragrant—though I know I won't be able to eat it. I leave the other pie where it is for now.

On Monday morning, I meet with my lawyer, Jim L., to "go over," as he says, "the rest of it." I can't get used to his office: a splendidly dark and glossy leather-and-mahogany sanctuary, where he spends his days forever in the eye of a storm. When I tell him about Sara coming with pies, how I didn't let her in, he proclaims, "Good!" His tone is simultaneously decisive and relieved. It's as if we'd dodged a bullet.

On Tuesday morning, I meet with Tracy, my counselor, as usual. Her office is a converted back porch, with leaded windows all around. My seat is a pew-like bench, strewn with huge, loose pillows, which I can hunker down in for one blessed hour each week. There's a catalpa tree out back I like to gaze at, the kind with long brown pods that crack each spring and release their spinning, double-winged seeds in any bit of breeze. When I tell her about the pies, Tracy beams, says, "Good! Thank *God*." But it's not as if we'd dodged a bullet. It's as if we've made great progress

As for me, I'm not so sure. I wonder if I'll ever be sure. Whether love is uplifting or not, is healthy and sane and wholesome or not, it's still the threshold of eternity, the closest most of us ever come. How can we walk away from it?

AMSTERDAM

[*March*]

1. Traveling

It's spring break. I'm standing in front of Amsterdam's Central Station, a little to the side because of the throngs flowing in and out. I watch trams filter toward me through an overhead space of wires and suspended lamp globes. They gather before the station, drop off a few people, and pull away to the right. I take my time. I'm jetlagged in the pale mid-morning. The ocean at my back, the city rays out all around, a baroque skyline of marquees, towers, and gilt domes wrapped around the center, where I stand with nowhere in particular to go.

What am I doing here? Back in Wilmington, with the first big court date for my divorce looming, all I'd wanted was an ocean behind me. But now that I've cashed in my Frequent Flyer miles, flown all night and disembarked at Schiphol, I suddenly wonder why I've chosen Amsterdam. It seemed to make sense a few days ago. It was one of the few great European cities I'd never visited. I'd always imagined it as Oz, although crisscrossed with canals.

Maybe it was an escapist fantasy that guided me here, or perhaps some deeper instinct. In any case, my life is about to change and by an unexpected route: through looking at old Dutch paintings. I have never formally studied art, but I've always loved to look at it. And as a young boy, I habitually lost myself in artistic efforts: drawings and watercolors, landscapes and seascapes. Sometimes I wonder if I might've become an artist, rather than a writer. In any case, I knew Amsterdam's Rijksmuseum was the home of many Rembrandts. But Rembrandt won't figure in my story; the transformation ahead of me will come courtesy of Johannes Vermeer.

I step out into the flow of crowds slowly drifting from square to square. In a corner breakfast bar, I choose a round *stroopwafel* from a glass decanter, dip the caramel-filled edge of it into black coffee, munch dreamily for a moment, then pocket the rest for later. I buy a canal tour-boat ticket—then climb into the long, bus-like contraption that barely slithers beneath each hump-backed sandstone bridge. We trace the rings of canals—the Kaizersgracht, the Prinsengracht—around the arc of the city. I look where I am pointed to look: *There* is the door of the Anne Frank House. *There*, at the corner, is the Westerkerk. See the yellow royal crown on the tower? *There* is the—

After only a few minutes, I start to grow weary of looking at the city like this, so I disembark at one of the stone landings, heavily climb the steps and cross a street. Almost immediately, I'm lost in the emerald vastness of the Museumplein, my backpack seemingly filled with rocks. A reflecting pool as long as a football field, a Ferris wheel beside it; the opera house and the Rijksmuseum lined up to face each other from afar at either end. The main gate of the Rijksmuseum is fenced off for renovations. I circle around to the temporary entrance on one end, and note tomorrow's visiting hours, nine to six.

I head back toward the center of this city of bridges, each arching its back beneath me as I cross. Atop each bridge, the black iron railings torque like tortuously braided tree roots. Down along the Flower Market on the Singel, barges and stalls with baskets of blossoms—a little early for tulips, but here are the deep-lit hues of crocuses and daffodils. I ghost through half-real squares with working jugglers, mimes, and every sort of street life or street theater imaginable.

Dog-tired at the center of town, my elbows propped on yet another bridge-railing, I gaze down yet another canal. Here, I'm transfixed by the lovely reflections, caught in the black waters, of the magenta fluorescent tubes that outline the windows on both sides. Evening throngs mill through the chill March air, past wigged man-nequin displays in fetish boutiques, coffee shops, and the upscale live-sex theaters. De Wallen. Here and here and here are the window girls, done up as satin black thong fantasies, or as schoolgirl-plaid-skirt fantasies, or simply as generic blondes. Some sway or swish to their iPods, half-heartedly baiting the waters, hands braced at the corners of the window frames. Some sit on pedestal stools while talking on cells or smoking. Here is a middle-aged fraulein in garters, with a crop tucked under one arm and an open sneer for every son-of-a-bitch who passes.

It's the fleshpot of fleshpots, a stone's throw from the harbor, so even the drunkest sailor couldn't miss it. But there are no drunken sailors now.

With surprising clarity, I remember certain scenes from my years in the Navy–paradise alleys in the depths of San Juan, Rota, Barcelona, all of the classic Sixth Fleet liberty ports. I had left my father's house, in Columbia, Missouri, the day after high school graduation, drifted for a few months, worked odd jobs in the Rockies, and then enlisted. It's difficult enough to simply be eighteen, but when you're eighteen and knotted up within yourself in the foul, hot hold of a steam-driven ship for months on end, those smoke-filled mercies—brothels and hovels stocked with neighborhood-sweetheart, twenty-buck whores—shine bright in the mind, like the final proof of God.

I remember riding the liberty launch into the Bay of Naples. 1975. The crew of my ship, the amphibious attack ship USS *El Paso,* had just rescued a thousand American civilians from the siege of Beirut. First, we spent a month anchored off shore in mined waters, waiting for negotiations that ultimately broke down. Suddenly one night we got the call, and went in thundering fast and hard with landing craft. A small band of Marines picked up the Americans in front of the embassy, and led them in single file down to the boats. From there, we delivered them—crowded on every deck, like anxious immigrants, each with a single suitcase—to Cyprus. It was our moment, our single, incandescent moment. Gerald Ford telephoned—patched in live, on the intercom—to thank us.

Then we approached fleet landing, under a flame-clear sky, bouncing through a little harbor chop. We could see the queue of girls on the pier, dolled up in heels and fishnet in broad daylight, late sun shadowing the immolated backdrop of Castel Nuovo. To the victors go the spoils.

Now, on the bridge, in this other liberty port, I hear a titter from behind as two women pass arm-in-arm. Normal, urban ladies, with scarves and topcoats. "Oh no, you would *not*," one says. "Would *so*." They are Brits, about my age. They're starting to gray but are still spritely, you might say, enjoying themselves immensely. Girls' night out.

For me, what the red lights of De Wallen signify is theme-park or "cultural tourist" lust and, charming as it is, there's little heat in it, for me. I'm far more tempted by the clink of glasses, laughter from every corner brewpub. I'm imagining a frothy swallow of Heineken, so I keep moving, moving, shivering, my mouth watering, and I don't stop.

Hours later, out of the wrong direction, I arrive on the waterfront, where I'd marked an *X* for the Renaissance Hotel on my map. It's a modern high-rise, earthen and mahogany tones inside. My room is on the fourth floor. I swing open the French windows to a canal view of gray sky, lead-gray water. Only eight o'clock, but I'm truly done—and lonelier than I've felt in years.

What am I doing here? I slump in the chair for half an hour without moving. In the bathroom, I line up pill bottles and inhalers on the sink—my Advair, Wellbutrin, Lexapro, Aleve—then sleep in my clothes until sunrise.

2. Daydreaming

There's a story I sometimes tell my college students about how I was placed in "slow" classes in grade school, a designation that lasted through high school. The reason, I think, was because I was extraordinarily shy and inward, and always traveling in my mind. I can conjure up my experience in a single scene. I remember an open window beside me, with a view across the emerald football field, its white chalked lines and wooden bleachers, and beyond that, nothing but rolling hills. I'd stare and stare, in a trance-like state, as the teacher's voice washed unintelligibly over me—as soothing as ocean waves, I might say now, though I never saw the ocean in my childhood. If I retained nothing from Basic Math or Wood Shop, at least I became a world-class dreamer.

The only event that had much impact on the reveries of my youth was the rather violent break-up of my family when I was thirteen. There were five children: three boys, then two girls. I was the second. For many months (it seemed forever), leading up to the split, there'd been nightly screams and threats and shattered plates and smashed furniture. Upstairs, in my bed, I tried covering my ears with my pillow. This break-up didn't disturb my inwardness so much as drive me deeper and more sullenly within myself. I even began using my alleged "slowness" as a crutch, an excuse for the daydreaming that was my principal survival mechanism.

At that time, my father, a biochemist, accepted a yearlong visiting position at the University of North Carolina at Chapel Hill. There were rumors of another woman. At the end of the year, when he finally showed up one day unannounced at our house, my mother attacked him with his own golf clubs, shattering most of the glass in his car before he managed to back out of the driveway.

After the divorce and after my father had returned to Missouri, my mother tried several times to force him to take me. What she said was that she couldn't afford to feed five children on a music teacher's salary. What I heard was that she didn't want me. He didn't want me, either. And I didn't want to go with him. Several times that year, my mother made me ask him. She'd dial his number, then hand over the heavy black receiver. He always said: Tell her no.

One Friday afternoon, in April, my mother suggested we go for a drive. I had just turned thirteen, so I presumed the outing had something to do with my birthday. But when we approached her red VW convertible, I saw, with a sinking feeling, that my thin twin mattress was stuck implausibly in the back of it.

"Wait, why is my mattress in the car?" I asked.

"Don't worry," she said, "we're getting you a new one." *Okay,* I thought. We rode for a mile or two, through newer and newer suburbs, she with an odd smile frozen on her face.

"Look at that beautiful lake," she said, as if I'd never seen Fairview Lake before.

Finally, she pulled into a strange apartment complex with a small parking lot. "Get out and help me with this mattress," she said. We unloaded it at the edge of the lot. "Better drag it over there onto the grass," she said.

While I was doing that, I glanced up just in time to see her duck back into the car.

"No," I pleaded. "Don't."

I stood behind the car to block her from backing out. She shifted into first gear, and drove forward over the curb. I remember how she glanced back once, with that same paralyzed smile, then jounced downhill across the lawn, and back to the street again.

This was the first time I'd seen where my father lived, in a modest brick four-plex. I sat on the curb, completely desolate, and waited a couple of hours for him to return home from his lab on the University of Missouri campus. He always worked late, six days a week.

Finally, at six p.m., he pulled into the parking lot, walked past me wordlessly, unlocked the back door of his ground-floor apartment, and disappeared inside. I waited another minute before I followed him.

He didn't kick me out; he knew he couldn't.

Back when the family was still together, my father kept a heavy, pigskin razor strop hanging on its own nail in the kitchen. Spankings were carried out with a grim sense of ceremony; the other children had to stand and watch. Probably this wasn't too unusual in those days, nor was it what made me resist living with him after the divorce. What I resisted was his silence. He simply didn't converse with his children. In the next few years I spent with him, he'd come home late, fix a martini, and that was pretty much it.

My father had many fine qualities: a relentless imagination and a stunning array of interests, from progressive politics to gardening to classical music to avant-garde film. I could say much the same of my mother, a classical violist and lifelong music teacher. But neither had much aptitude for parenting.

That's why I enlisted. It turned out there were two and only two aspects of the Navy that suited me: drinking and traveling. Because I continued to drink like a sailor after my discharge, I ended up in recovery a few years later. That was almost twenty-five years ago. I've yet to find a reason to stop traveling.

3. Why, Why

The next morning, I drop in at a MacBike location a block from my hotel, rent a big, black clunker, and head off for the Rijksmuseum. In the Philips Wing, an exhibition of seventeenth-century paintings, "The Masterpieces," is on temporary display. The rest of the museum is undergoing its long-anticipated renovation, or reincarnation. The show is a best-hits narrative, culminating in Rembrandt's colossal *Night Watch,* always the crown jewel here. In seventeen rooms, the show sketches the explosion of secular art: portrait, still life, seascape, genre scene. The twenty Rembrandts, including the great *The Jewish Bride,* are arrayed in the two galleries toward the end. The latter is a picture of a somewhat older couple (perhaps Isaac and Rebecca), clasping each other solemnly. It's as arresting for its splendid golden textures and hallowed light, as for its subject; it makes me realize how rare it is to see such a sincere celebration, without a tinge of irony, of older adults in love.

Along the way, there are a couple of smaller rooms devoted to groups of paintings by Jan Steen and Johannes Vermeer. Because there are so many Rembrandts to see, I decide to give the Vermeer room only a minute or two. I stop and gaze down the length of the space; three works by the Delft master hang on the far wall. (A fourth appears with related genre works—busy group scenes—on the right-hand wall.) The Vermeers are unexpectedly small, but the force of the spell they cast is so eerily powerful that it's difficult to move, to breathe.

So I stop, I look around. The walls are cream-colored floral damask; the floor is parquet, with a centered, rectangular, slate blue rug. Behind me: Gabriel Metsu's frankly disturbing yet sympathetic *The Sick Child*. I take a step or two toward the small Vermeer on the wall to my right: it's called *The Love Letter*. Revealed through a dark doorway is a complicated scene. A well-dressed lady, holding a lute (I think), receives, over her shoulder, the eponymous letter from her maid. The room they are in is opulent, filled with bourgeois clutter (a laundry basket, a broom, a crumpled sheet of music). There's a sense of withheld meaning in this painting—withheld from me— and it doesn't attract me.

I move ahead to the Vermeers on the far wall. *The Milkmaid* is in the center. On the left is a cityscape, *The Little Street*. On the right is the pensive *Woman in Blue Reading a Letter*. But it is *The Milkmaid* that stuns from a distance, drawing my eyes magnetically to the lowered eyes of the woman, her shadow incised against the luminous whitewash. I feel a shiver all the way up and down my spine.

She stands before a still life of bread crusts and basket, pouring a steady trickle of milk from an earthenware pitcher into a bowl—a slip of motion at the heart of so much stillness. Her form is startling, hyper-real: the vivid lemon-yellow tunic balanced against the lapis lazuli depths of her skirts. Likewise, the tight weave of the wicker basket; cool, crisp, linen bonnet; nubby tunic. Stillness. Not emptiness but stillness, a great soul balanced there.

I'm drawn to her broad and ruddy brow—built up laboriously of heavy, individual strokes of impasto that remain unmixed—but also to the wall behind her. It is a coarse, workaday wall, befitting the painting's subject and memorable for its grittiness, its lovingly pockmarked patina. Above and to the left of the maid's face are trompe-l'oeil nails with nail-heads and, most startlingly, the shadows of the nails, fixed in the plaster. The light falls from the left onto the maid's chest, bordering her right side in deep shade. By dramatically brightening the wall to her right, which, in a more realistic painting, would be in shadow, Vermeer defines her by contrast. A thin, white line, outlining her right side and sculpting her almost into relief, heightens this effect. The calculation, the trickery is nearly invisible; the image ravishes. After a few minutes, I move left, sidestepping the steady throng *The Milkmaid* attracts.

The Little Street is also a hymn to the domestic, a representative view of Delft—a long, slow, cloud-banked afternoon, such as Vermeer must have seen, at any given moment, through his studio window. A couple of women, glimpsed through open doorways, go about their chores; two children crouch beneath a bench outside, utterly absorbed in some game of their own. Between the roofs of the two main houses, at the front of the painting, is a V of skyline, with grayish, thinly painted chimneys receding into the scumbled distance. A few tendrils of ivy cling to the front of the cottage at left, convincing, yet of a weird, almost neon-blue. (I'll discover later that this is a fairly common occurrence in Dutch painting; the loss of the surface yellow glaze turns the natural ultramarine green to blue.)

Some details, like the thicket of chimneys, are quick strokes on the canvas. Others are exquisitely realistic, like the watery striations in the cobbles, the whitewashed brick around each doorway. I love how the whitewash extends only as high as a man could conveniently reach, and the way the shutters on the right-hand house grow more sun-faded as the eye moves from the first to the third floor. Tributaries of cracks in the fascia angle down the grain of the brickwork, roughly patched with mortar. There's something deeply familiar, deeply felt, about this vision of the taken-for-granted, wear-and-tear of time. On the one hand, there's a light touch that makes more recent eras of realism plod by comparison. On the other, the faithfulness of the eye and the brush makes the blurry effects of Impressionism seem a little callow. It is a style as much unconscious as conscious—and blessedly free of sentiment—as if a caul had suddenly lifted, allowing the eye to meet the world.

With some effort, I pull away, and skirt around to the right of *The Milkmaid,* to *Woman in Blue Reading a Letter*. It is a later work (c. 1662–1665), though not as late as *The Love Letter* (c. 1667–1670). The differences between *Woman in Blue Reading a Letter* and the two earlier works are unsettling. The softly shadowed side of the woman's face is indistinguishable in color from the shadowy contour map that undulates directly behind her; it is of Holland, though I'd only discover this later, in art books. The vision is all softness, tones of sepia and cerulean. In certain passages, like the front and sleeve of the ultramarine blouse, highlights are laved in gold. Along the plaster wall, which glows pale-gold, shadows are tinted blue.

Unlike the gritty backdrop for the woman in *The Milkmaid*—which is as luminous and detailed as possible—there is no sense of perspective supporting this carefully coifed but solitary blue letter-reader. She floats in the currents of her own space, with nothing to fix her among the nebulous hues of the plaster, the umber terra incognita of the map. What we see of her form—her neck, her forearms—is elegantly pale and long, though her body seems to swell at the waist; whether this is due to a pregnancy, or to the belled style of the dress, I can't decide.

I remember Elizabeth Bishop's poem "The Moose," which describes a memory of a childhood voyage, a night-time bus trip. The bus stops because a "grand, otherworldly" moose has appeared in the middle of the moonlit road. Then, taking its time, the moose inspects the bus, and the speaker whispers:

> Why, why do we feel
> (we all feel) this sweet
> sensation of joy?

Why do I feel this sweet sensation of joy? I look from one painting to the next: the little street, the milkmaid, and the letter reader. For the moment, I am this tingling at the back of my scalp.

4. *The Flash*

I walk ahead through late, dark Rembrandt, and then loop back to Vermeer again. I browse through elegant De Hooch—his open doorways, merry companies—then return to Vermeer again. Finally,

I move on to the heavily guarded, sea-green room that houses Rembrandt's masterpiece commonly known as *The Night Watch* (actually titled *The Company of Frans Banning Cocq and Willem van Ruytenburch*). Its size and splendor is a shock. Fourteen feet wide, it seethes with national pride. The captain and his lieutenant are lit at the center with dramatic chiaroscuro, as is a little girl, part mascot, part guardian angel. Behind and around the three, an entire militia prepares for a peacetime parade, though for all the Baroque bravado of musket and lance, they might as well be readying to die for the common good. Here I stop.

I've seen enough, the exit beckons, but something has happened. Instead of leaving, I turn and float lightheaded against the press of the crowd, back through the galleries to the Vermeer room again.

Then I stand before the sunlit street, the milkmaid, and the letter reader. I'm thinking now with my eyes, my skin, I'm drifting sidelong into dream—the paintings meet me there. I feel the trickle of memory in the street's gutter. There is the doe-faced maid at the center of it all, ministering forever. There is the cloud-blue reader, dissolving in the raptness of her attention.

I'm standing well back in the center of the room. People move quietly toward the paintings. Each person whispers, in German or Japanese; some say nothing at all.

Suddenly, I understand: Vermeer's hushed clarity addresses me, is *for* me as I stand here now. What I've been going through, what I've tried to deal with in my divorce, is total loss. I thought I knew about all that when my first wife, Jackie, died of cancer—but this time, I 'd lost faith. It isn't just that I don't believe in love; I'm not sure I believe in anything. But, looking at these radiant canvases— unreachable yet familiar—reminds me. The rapturous inner life of each woman and the infinitesimally detailed and self-contained life of the street are each imagined as an undiscovered heaven on earth. It's as if these visions are here to startle me to my senses by showing me recovered images from a former life.

Now I leave and retrace my steps through the rooms. On the white marble stairway, I reach for the sharp-edged, stainless-steel handrail. A shape flits before me, inside me, in my mind—an abstract shape like a helix, like the arc of a swallow's flight. I reach the landing, and turn.

All this takes place in a moment: one prolonged flash.

When I was ten or eleven, on a cold gray autumn day, my older brother Dan took me outside and unwrapped a foot-long ribbon of magnesium. (Because my father tended to bring his work home with him, our house back then was a wonderland of beakers and Bunsen burners, microscopes, pipettes, and other paraphernalia.) He let me hold it, weightless and malleable in my hands. Then he solemnly went through a vaguely scientific process of sparking a propane torch, fine-tuning its flame—as Dad had taught him— and lighting the coiled magnesium on our gravel drive. It burned spookily, with a godlike, white-blue flame that Dan said we were not supposed to look at. When he threw a cup of water on it, it sputtered noxiously, then leapt up violently, so we flinched and scattered. Soon, though, it petered out, and we were left to marvel at its spiral spine of ash.

The eerie, inexplicable intensity I feel when looking at Vermeer's paintings is like that—that different kind of fire. A certain chain of events has left me open, on a startlingly deep level, to Vermeer's gaze, to his meditation on our place on earth.

There are only thirty-five Vermeers in the world. How many cities house groups of them? Not more than a handful, I'm pretty sure. I could see most of the oeuvre in a matter of months. I'll use every break from school, travel from city to city, museum to museum. And because of the light that Amsterdam and the Rijksmuseum has shed on Vermeer, this visit will be the model for the rest.

5. Itinerary

Outside, sitting on a black metal bench with a Vermeer catalog, my Marble notebook and Uniball pen in hand, I come up with an itinerary. It starts here in Amsterdam, and will take a little more than a year.

AMSTERDAM
(Rijksmuseum)
The Little Street (c. 1657–1661)
The Milkmaid (c. 1658–1661)
Woman in Blue Reading a Letter (c. 1662–1665)
The Love Letter (c. 1667–1670)

THE HAGUE
(Mauritshuis)
The Girl with a Pearl Earring (c. 1665–67)
View of Delft (c. 1660–61)
Diana and Her Companions (c. 1653–56)

WASHINGTON, D.C.
(The National Gallery)
Girl with a Red Hat (c. 1665–1667)
Girl Holding a Flute (c. 1664–1665)
Woman Holding a Balance (c. 1662–1665)
A Lady Writing (c. 1665–1666)

NEW YORK
(The Frick Collection)
Officer and Laughing Girl (c. 1655–1660)
Girl Interrupted in Her Music (c. 1656–1661)
Mistress and Maid (c. 1666–1667)

(The Metropolitan Museum of Art)
A Maid Asleep (c. 1656–1657)
Young Woman with a Water Pitcher (c. 1664–1665)
Study of a Young Woman (c. 1665–1674)
Woman with a Lute (c. 1662–1664)
Allegory of Faith (c. 1670–1674)

LONDON
(The Kenwood House)
The Guitar Player (c. 1670–1672)

(The Royal Collection)
The Music Lesson (c. 1662–1664)

(The National Gallery)
A Lady Standing at a Virginal (c. 1670–1673)
A Lady Seated at a Virginal (c. 1670–1675)

6. *The Toast*

Early evening: I clatter up to my hotel and, in the alley, lock my black bike to a handy railing. Inside, my room is fresh and cool because I have left the windows open all day. A relaxed café buzz wafts in, through the billowing curtains, up from the canal-front streets below. I unload my backpack onto my bed. I've stopped at the Aelbert Cuyp street-market on the way home and filled my panniers at the fish-stalls and cheese-stalls. A wedge of smoky Gouda; a round of Leiden peppered with cumin seeds; a whole smoked herring wrapped in butcher-paper; a jar of brine-cured, purplish Calamata olives; two shriveled Italian salamis; a crusty loaf in its brown paper sleeve; a few Sanguineli oranges; a small box of Belgian chocolates wrapped in golden foil. I arrange all this on the tiny, round pedestal table next to the open window. I raise a glass of mineral water to the Amsterdam skyline, and then saw into the hard cheeses and pungent, wild boar salamis as best I can with a sterling butter knife. I'm famished; I tear the rinds with my teeth, can't get enough.

Later, after a hot shower, I wipe a clearing in the mirror and take a long look. I'd like to say I see my father's son, the handsome sailor, hiding beneath this grizzled forehead with eyes askew, this crooked and dented nose, but I don't. It's just a middle-aged guy, a recovering drunk, who looks look pretty tired and old. Still, as if a broken heart were something like a hangover, I try to focus myself. I pick up the bottle of Lexapro, unscrew the cap, and pour the contents into the toilet.

THE HAGUE AND DELFT

[June]

1. *The Girl*

Another turbulent red-eye flight to Schiphol, and once again, I haven't slept. The countryside steams by in the sun as I roll seaward in a sunflower-yellow local train, past the ungainly windmills, flooded polders, village after village. Past sheep and goats and swans and geese. It's green-gold June. I've been reading travel books in preparation for my return. Watching the vista unspool with its relentless flatness—the view unimpeded in every direction and dwarfed by the towering sky above—I understand why there are four Dutch nouns for *horizon,* although I can't recall them now. A second later, I realize I've missed the tulip season by a couple of weeks. Empty field after empty field files past, precisely measured and orderly.

One month ago my father passed away. Back in Missouri, on his way to church one afternoon, he was T-boned by a young man driving a big F-250. Nothing I could do, the young man said. My father remained in a coma for several days and never regained consciousness. His sons and daughters, all five of us, gathered at his bedside and made a difficult decision on his behalf. Faced with another hard loss without respite, all I can decide to do is press on with Vermeer.

In The Hague Central, I slide the handle out of my bag and wheel outside—past the happy couples checking their iPhones, looking for cabs—without the vaguest notion of where I'm going. I've only bumped along a few blocks, toward what seems the center of things, when I make out a two-story banner, draped down a building just across a square: an immense reproduction of *The Girl with a Pearl Earring.*

Night after night in my armchair, with art books or Vermeer studies open in my lap, I had looked at her face, the color plates cool beneath my fingertips. How odd it is to suddenly see her looming as big as a cloud above the treetops, the face I had dreamed of, that had lingered in my mind for weeks, like the Cheshire Cat. My path couldn't have been more direct, over the ocean and through the streets, and suddenly here I am. I'm raw, as expectant as a pilgrim.

The Mauritshuis (the Dutch Royal Gallery) houses two of Vermeer's masterpieces, *The Girl with a Pearl Earring* and *View of Delft*, as well as an example of his juvenilia, the Italianate *Diana and Her Companions*. Much to my delight, it happens that one other masterpiece, not on my itinerary, is on loan from Vienna for one more day: his great studio scene, *The Art of Painting*.

I'm on my way to see Vermeer, floating up the red-carpeted stairs, in this high-ceilinged palace. Just before entering the Vermeer room, something catches my eye, just to the left of the oak doorframe. It's Carel Fabritius's trompe-l'oeil miniature, *The Goldfinch,* which I recognize from my reading (and which has not yet been made world-famous by Donna Tartt's novel of the same name). It's a painting of a domesticated goldfinch on an elaborate perch attached to a whitewashed wall, and the contrast between the off-center, startlingly realized bird and the softly glowing wall behind is striking. Fabritius was Rembrandt's student, and was later Vermeer's friend and/or mentor in Delft. Almost all of Fabritius's paintings were lost in the Delft Thunderclap of 1654, when a gunpowder explosion leveled much of the city. But *The Goldfinch,* especially—with its naturalism, cool sunlight, white backdrop, grittiness and ordinariness—seems essential to Vermeer. It's a prelude, a source for the poetry of Vermeer's solitary women.

Going into the room, the walls are a muted and patterned green—the light, which comes from the right as you walk in, is shuttered, the effect subaqueous. There's one painting on each wall. Vermeer's great landscape, *View of Delft*, is alone on the left wall, as luminous as a torch. But I also feel a breeze, a shiver on my back as I enter, causing me to turn to face *The Girl with a Pearl Earring,* to the right of the doorway. I look at her across my left shoulder. She is looking me dead in the eye across her own left shoulder. She is, if any painting ever can be, a breathtaking encounter.

Love: How could I have forgotten that feeling? The instantaneous, passionate gaze that comprehends me, beyond accusation or forgiveness. The lovely sympathy in her hazel irises, the lush eroticism of her lips, her mouth. She is the clapper, I am the bell, and she rings through my whole body.

2. The Earring

I look up, blink. A ray of sunlight has slipped through the shutters, fallen at my feet. Maybe a half-hour, maybe an hour has passed.

Nothing could've prepared me for the painting's hold on me. I've read about the sitter, who was probably Vermeer's daughter Maria, aged twelve or thirteen at the time, and I know the painting isn't a portrait, but is purposefully fantastical. I've read and reread the brilliant passages on this work by critics Lawrence Gowing and Edward Snow. But I hadn't expected this deep dream, this first and last love. It's all I can do to return her gaze.

The painting is much smaller than I'd expected: only about fifteen inches wide and eighteen inches tall. The badly abraded background—originally a deep, translucent green—is blackish, amorphous nothingness. Over the centuries, a fine eggshell craqueleur has developed across the entire surface and is far more extensive than you'd imagine from the digitized photos. I'm not sure these changes should even be regretted; the essence of the girl projected through the cracked, eroded surface seems undiminished. In fact, she seems all the more moving to me, all the more precious for her ability to transcend the ravages of age. Reproductions are useless, I suddenly think.

Directly across the room, *The Art of Painting* casts its own eerily magnetic spell. It is an enormous and deep studio scene depicting a seated painter's back (often considered a stand-in for Vermeer), as he, the painter, begins a painting of a smiling girl, who is standing in the flow of light, beyond and to the left. The model for the girl was probably the same as for *The Girl with a Pearl Earring*. She is fresh and pretty, with youthful, wide-set eyes. The painting is among the most allegorical of all Vermeer's works, which are seldom allegorical. The girl, wearing a laurel crown, represents Clio, goddess of history. The seated painter gazes at his comely model, his right hand sketching a few leaves from her wreath on his canvas. She doesn't return his attention, but gazes down mysteriously toward a white mask lying face-up on the table before her. The corner of the table points back toward the painter, nearly touches his hip. Looking into the depths of this painting is a little like gazing into a swirling snow globe, a self-sufficient cosmos.

Hanging on the rear wall in the painting is a large map of Holland, the most detailed of all of Vermeer's glorious maps, with truly photographic fidelity, complete with a convincing, dramatic crease that roughly corresponds to the North/South political split in the Netherlands. In between the wall and the viewer is indeterminate space. The shimmering, golden chandelier at top appears at first glance to be rendered in marvelously fine detail, but when I actually look at it, it is all highlight and shadow—heavy brushstrokes of cream defining sunlit surfaces—and little else.

I turn and look again at the earring in the painting of the girl behind me—that most celebrated detail—two spherical daubs of paint. One bright brush mark along the left-hand curve of the pearl reflects direct sunlight; and a fainter stroke (only recently revealed in cleaning) follows the bottom curve, and seems to be radiant light from her white collar. The body of the pearl filled in by desire, by dream—my desire, my dream.

3. Luminosity

Vermeer died abruptly in 1675, when he was forty-three and penniless, due to the collapsed art market. Catharina, his widow, described his death as follows: "As a result and owing to the great burden of his children, having no means of his own, he had lapsed into such decay and decadence, which he had so taken to heart that, as if he had fallen into a frenzy, in a day or day and a half had gone from being healthy to being dead."

It's difficult to know for certain what to make of that cryptic statement. But hard times were upon the Dutch, at war yet again, and the art market had evaporated in the widespread panic. As a result, Vermeer couldn't feed his large family—his wife and their eleven children—and when he died, he left them bankrupt. It's known that he kept *The Art of Painting* at home to the end, alone among all his works. Then, after the bankruptcy, Catharina faithfully attempted to safeguard the masterpiece from creditors by transferring ownership to her mother. However, it seems to have been sold at auction soon thereafter.

If *The Art of Painting* is a high water mark among Vermeer's interior scenes, *View of Delft* is anomalous. Without moving from my spot, I pivot left again, toward the *View*. As the only real landscape, it's an exception within a uniquely focused career, and absolutely shines in this room.

The high, swept sky, with its shadowy threat in the first bank of clouds above us and a brilliant whiteness of cirrus beyond, registers distance in brighter and brighter drifts of cloud above the North Sea. This big sky is dully mirrored in the bronze-green waters of the Schie, and it dazzles the eye with passages of distilled brilliance and my mind with memories of such brilliance. I hunch my shoulders; I even squint a little. Although facing a shuttered window in the wall directly across from it, the painting radiates; it is the light-source inside this physical space.

Beyond the radiance of the composition, I'm struck by the thickness of the paint. The clouds are laid in with the same heavy impasto technique Vermeer used for some of the whitewashed walls in his interiors, and for the face of *The Milkmaid*. The lead-white pigment of the period was unusually coarse (and prized for its coarseness), its grainy texture gathering points of reflected light. Vermeer also sometimes mixed sand into the paint (especially in the earlier work) to create texture and luminosity. Some highlights—like the bright yellow hue that adorns gables and walls in the townscape—are so built up, they glitter like a papier-mâché school project. The vision is lovingly layered and hewn, and it's even more startling to us now, accustomed as we are to processed paints and pigments. Marcel

Proust's *In Search of Lost Time* famously and enigmatically includes a passage about a "little patch of yellow wall" somewhere in this painting, like a "priceless specimen of Chinese art," which is the last thing the writer Bergotte looks at before he dies. No one knows for sure which patch of paint Proust meant.

And then there's the lovely, vaguely lonely feel of the town itself. The painting is composed of several bands: sky and city and water. The sky is the largest of these; beneath the sky is the narrow strip of city; then the bronze-green Kolk. And in the left foreground, on our side, there's part of the riverbank at our feet, with a moored ferry and several people. Two women stand off on their own, talking. They're wearing peasant dresses, black with white collars. One holds a basket.

What we see of the town, across the water, is mostly waterfront—the outer walls and gates with rooftops and towers above—and in the center glows one particular sunlit fold of buildings. We're actually looking across the Schie, straight up the mouth of the main canal that divides, just after the bridge, to become Delft's principal arteries, the Oude Delft and the Nieuwe Delft. I can make out the bridge, the city wall, two entrances on the southern end—the Rotterdam Gate and the Schiedam Gate—and then, beyond, a slice of the interior: a couple of steeples and roofs, and not much else. The scene is gorgeously, fervently colored—blood-red roofs on the left, deep ochre on the right—passionate, yet thoroughly bourgeois. The Nieuwe Kerk steeple is sculpted in startlingly heavy impasto. A tiny clock on the Schiedam Gate reads a few minutes past seven. There are fifteen (tiny) human figures in the painting, I've read, but it looks almost empty to me.

The nearer parts of the town are shadowed by the storm clouds directly above, but there's a clearing behind the darkness where a ray of sun breaks through. I can't see this ray itself, only its effect on the sunlit interior of the painting. The Nieuwe Kerk steeple is fully, perhaps symbolically lit—it's the brightest spot—probably because William of Orange is buried there. This great national hero, who led the Dutch revolt against the occupying Spanish, was assassinated in 1584. Vermeer's spotlighting of the Nieuwe Kerk, then, was a patriotic homage, which wouldn't be missed by any Dutch eye. Most striking to me, however, is the simple fact, the feeling, of the sunlit center. I sense the stir of human activity (the Nieuwe Kerk is on the market square), the day about to begin, the blessing of light. The town is neither idealized nor abstracted, neither larger nor smaller than it needs to be, and one cannot know what God thinks about it.

The waters of the Schie were widened, in 1614, into a triangular harbor called the Kolk. Some experts think the standpoint for *View of Delft* was the upper floor of a house, long gone, that stood on the bank. There, at his leisure, Vermeer would have set up his camera obscura, which would cast its image either onto a wall or into a darkened box. This image could then be directly transcribed, and worked into a painting later.

These optical details fascinate us now; originality and "authenticity" are special concerns of our age. Would we look differently on the *Mona Lisa* if we learned that she hadn't been painted from nature, but traced from a projected image? Perhaps. In any case, David Hockney and Philip Steadman have argued that Vermeer used a camera as a matter of course, that he probably learned about optics from his peer Antony van Leeuwenhoek, the self-taught Delft scientist and inventor of the microscope. Steadman's main purpose, in his book *Vermeer's Camera*, is to show that some of Vermeer's compositions *must* have been created by optical means. There's really no other plausible explanation for the accuracy of detail, he argues, for the way such infinitesimally complex tile patterns, for instance, continue uninterruptedly on either side of a table or chair.

And *View of Delft*, with its luminous clarity, does imply the use of a camera, or some such setup in the house across the Kolk. The townscape is abruptly "cropped" on the sides, an effect that would have been quite shocking then. This cropping would make sense if, and perhaps only if, Vermeer's compositions had been framed by a lens.

And then there's the effect often called "circles of confusion," or pointillés: spherical daubs of luminous paint. These highlights resemble the optical effects produced by a lens, especially by the imperfect, hand-ground lenses of the day. For example, on the

right-hand side of the canvas, across the Schie, there are two herring boats moored for repairs. In an otherwise meticulously realistic
scene, the pointillés are pure poetic embellishment—scattered flakes
of gold that follow the shadowy contours of the hulls, the seams
of the planking, the gunwales. They are strewn lavishly through
shadows and luminous areas alike, and the eye simply accepts their
presence. Vermeer's most penetrating critic, Lawrence Gowing,
describes this phenomenon as a glittering "commentary of light."

Another peculiar decision that Vermeer makes in his signature
landscape involves perspective. He places the largest possible body
of water between himself and his subject. He chooses distance; he
makes what is most familiar to him unfamiliar. He portrays the
Kolk—a significant harbor in the seventeenth-century—early in
the morning, and nearly vacant. This reminds me of Wordsworth's
sublime but slightly strained sonnet "Composed Upon Westminster
Bridge, September 3, 1802," which describes smoke-choked nineteenth-century London with an oddly pastoral rhetoric: "This City
now doth, like a garment, wear / The beauty of the morning; silent,
bare . . ." Both artists show us their cities in the best possible light,
but they have to get up pretty early to do so.

But is the essence remoteness or unknowability? There's nothing remote about *The Girl with a Pearl Earring*—the exquisite maid
who stands frozen, Eurydice-like, in a welter of conflicting passions.
She couldn't stand any closer to me; her clear gaze couldn't seize me
more directly.

Whether she's turning toward or away from me, though, I don't
know. Impossible to know whether she's turning toward or away
from the nothingness behind her.

In *View of Delft*, the comings and goings of men and women
are dwarfed by a not altogether friendly sky. But what is realized is
thrillingly realized—if from across the water—the city vibrant with
gold and russet. Again and again, I'm overcome by desire to enter
that city.

I stay in the Mauritshuis another hour, as my ability to concen-
trate comes and goes—and finally goes for good. In the cozy museum

cafeteria, in the basement, I sit quietly, hoping a frothy double espresso can revive me. It doesn't. I'm crashing, the long trip catching up with me. It feels like the weight of divorce, jet lag, and the peculiar loneliness of travel are suddenly bearing down. I nod, shudder with two or three convulsive yawns, and realize I have to leave.

4. Dr. Kees Kaldenbach

It looks, it feels like the first true summer afternoon of the year as I pedal through Amsterdam's idyllic Vondelpark. It's Wednesday, the day before I'm traveling to Delft. I'm on my way to meet an art historian, Dr. Kees Kaldenbach, who lives a couple of blocks from the park's south gate. He's one of the best living critics of Vermeer's work, and probably knows more about Delft, as Vermeer knew it, than anyone.

Dr. Kaldenbach opens the door. He's shy and lanky, looming above me as he ushers me into a large, high-ceilinged living room filled with art books and houseplants. He's awkward and tentative and repetitive in his movements. After offering me a drink (I ask for ice water, which baffles him. "Are you sure?" he asks), he makes a couple of protracted trips to the kitchen before informing me, with a vague wave of the hand, that the freezer is "defrosting."

Finally, he manages to provide a glass of slightly cool tap water, and sits down next to me on the sofa. I've come armed with a few questions but can't seem to articulate what I was thinking. I go ahead and try anyway. How much of a given work is "observed," I wonder, how much "improvised"? Are there patterns, tendencies he can tell me about? But I realize it's probably impossible to answer, and tell Kaldenbach so. He nods.

We flip through a glossy book of Vermeer reproductions, until we light on *View of Delft*. I touch it with my fingertips, and ask if I will be able to see the view, the standpoint from which Vermeer painted, when I go to Delft. Is it still there, or has the city changed too much? "It's there," he says. Quickly, he sketches out, with a slender index finger, how much of the actual painting I'll be able to see as Vermeer saw it. Steeples, one or two particular roofs, here and here and here. How accurate was Vermeer in his portrayal of the town? "*Very* accurate," says Kaldenbach. He notes how the two herring buses—fishing boats—are riding unusually high in the water, moored for repairs. The fact that both are missing their masts. Why would he make a choice like that? Would a painter choose to paint two sailboats without their masts if he were not painting from life?

But I had read, I say, that Vermeer had altered the profile of the town for dramatic effect. That maybe the painting isn't a literal representation. Kaldenbach nods: "It's a *photoshop*." Certain details are exaggerated. The Nieuwe Kerk steeple, for example, is much taller, more prominent in the painting than it ought to be. What *is* true about the view, however, is uncannily true. So true, in fact, that Kaldenbach has recently dated the composition of this painting to 1660–61 based on the boat traffic depicted and also on the absence of bells in the Nieuwe Kerk, which were removed then and later replaced by the famous Hemony brothers, whose cast bells were installed in churches throughout Europe.

I ask if Vermeer used the camera obscura. Kaldenbach believes he did, but that Steadman "goes too far." He says, "I think Vermeer used it to capture ideas," but he didn't slavishly copy what he saw.

We talk about the many ways in which Vermeer violates what might be thought of as the literal "reality" of a scene. For instance, in *The Art of Painting*, he points out how the size difference between the two figures, the male painter and female model, is not nearly as great as it ought to be in perspective, with the model at the back of the room, the painter in the middle.

At heart, according to Kaldenbach, Vermeer's process is typical for Dutch painters. He explains how the vanishing point of many of Vermeer's interiors is marked with a tiny pinhole, which you can see in many of the canvases, if you look closely. Kaldenbach points out where it is, exactly, in *The Milkmaid*, just above the maid's right hand, which holds the pitcher. Vermeer, like other Dutch painters (whom the Italians, with their refined laws of perspective, considered crude), used a simple chalk line, a pin with a chalked string attached, to check his perspectives. Plucking the string—I imagine the pop, I smell the tiny cloud of chalk-dust—he could trace the vanishing lines directly onto the canvas.

Kaldenbach tells me how Vermeer experimented with the act, as he puts it, of "looking/encoding into paint/seeing what happens when decoding." He says, "Vermeer is not interested in what he knows, but in what he sees." He says that Vermeer finds "new pathways" in the process of encoding/decoding—his move toward abstraction is one of the great examples. It begins about the time of *View of Delft,* shortly after *The Little Street.*

The Little Street, especially, is breathtakingly representational— Anthony Bailey, for instance, lauds its "wonderful plausibility." Its brushwork manages to lend individual bricks and individual leaves a graceful presence and weight. But a great change has occurred by *View of Delft,* which involves not only optical effects like the pointillés, but what Kaldenbach calls Vermeer's "mosaic of abstractions." The roofs are undifferentiated shapes; flat, tonal values that we read intuitively as *things.* The painting lifts off, lifts away. The site where the decoding takes place seems to be redefined (as it would be again by the Impressionists). His work grows calm; the paint is thinner, the brushwork less descriptive, more calligraphic. This trend culminates triumphantly in the abstract, Matisse-like style shown in the Vermeers in our National Gallery, coming up soon in my itinerary.

The interview takes maybe an hour. By then I have run out of questions. What I realize is that I haven't come looking for answers. I'm trying to enter Vermeer's world, so I'm here to meet the inhabitants. I find Kaldenbach easy and pleasant to sit with.

Then I turn to the *View* again. It has been called a "hymn" to civic pride and the like, but it seems to me to get at something much more basic—a serene, unrepeatable vision of our place, our existence on earth. I ask Kaldenbach if the painting is essentially Dutch in some way, or is it more "universal"? He exclaims, without hesitation, stabbing his finger emphatically at it: "Well, this painting could not have been painted in any other country! Look at it: it is sixty percent sky. *Our* clouds. *Our* reflections."

We sit another moment. Finally I rise to go, and he escorts me out onto the quiet street. I'm beginning to unlock my bike from the lamppost, fumbling with the combination, when I think of one last thing.

"In *The Girl with a Pearl Earring,* is the girl turning toward or away from us?" I ask.

Kaldenbach looks befuddled, smiles and shrugs from his lofty height. "You can't be sure, it's impossible . . ."

I know, I want to say. For all the motion implied by her over-the-shoulder glance—by the out-flung headdress—it is only the fierce intensity of her glance that matters.

I shake his hand, swing my leg over the saddle, and push off round the corner, past a bus stop and a herring stand.

Then I pedal aimlessly through the undulant, nearly-wild byways of the Vondelpark—past clusters of slender young lovers draped over and over and over each other on blankets or on the grass, with guitars and bottles of wine or nothing but each other. I'm suddenly hitting a wall again. Jetlag slows the wheels of the wobbling bike, until I cross a footbridge, meander between two ponds full of swans, then tip over softly, as in a dream. I stretch out in a sunflower glade, and for the first time this year, I'm not wracked with anxiety over how things are going across the ocean—how I'm going to finish the divorce, yet forge a lasting relationship with my daughter—because the moment my head relaxes into the grass, I'm fast asleep.

5. *The View*

The doors of the Delft station open directly across from the original city, safe behind its ancient walls. It faces me broadside, two steeples in the center, with a fortified gate straight ahead. But instead of passing through and into the town, I turn right and follow the sidewalk around—outside the wall—toward the south end, holding a map half folded in one hand. The fact that Delft has changed so little has much to do with its attraction for me. It isn't about the town as much as the bricks, the canals, the skies. They are the same red bricks, tea-brown canals, and high white skies that colored every moment of Vermeer's life and art.

In five minutes, I reach the south end, the river Schie opening up on my right, a promenade running alongside. I figure this must be the harbor in the painting, but I'm not sure. At one end, there's a bridge to the other side, so I cross and walk along an embankment where a couple of yachts are moored. When I come to a turn—a little point projecting into the water—there's an unmarked, flowered terrace looking out on the town. On a small, grassy slope in front of the terrace, four teen-aged girls in bikinis lie sunbathing on towels. I kneel on the walk next to them and, feeling very sheepish, say "Hi," and then ask collectively, "Does anyone speak English?"

"A little," one girl says.

"Do you know if this is the place where Vermeer painted *View of Delft?*"

"Eh, Vermeer?" repeats one, cheerfully. She's freckled, looks sixteen, and has a mouthful of braces. I spread the map on the grass. An X marks the spot called "Delftview" on the map. Is this it? All four girls swarm about the map, talking all at once and pointing here and there at various landmarks. After a few minutes, as I see we're getting nowhere, I thank them profusely—they're really sweet. I step away and realize, after a moment, that it is. This has to be the standpoint.

Simon Schama thinks Vermeer had been forced to paint Delft from the south because the 1654 Thunderclap had leveled the entire northeast quarter. He doesn't entirely convince me. I can see that this prospect offers one enormous advantage to Vermeer: distance. Here, and only here, can we look at the city across the widest breadth of the Kolk. From this point, Delft might as well be an island.

The triangular Kolk spreads before me, in outline unchanged from the seventeenth-century, the two steeples in exactly the same positions across the water as in the painting. The water ripples, full of silvery reflections. On the right-hand side of the view is a traditional Dutch herring bus, moored in exactly the same place as the two in the painting. Its broad, rounded ends; clean whitewash; heavy, varnished mast; and especially, the archaic, varnished leeboards are the real thing. The sky is a bright and high-ceilinged North Sea sky, almost as dramatic as the one in the painting.

Otherwise, looking at the vista as it is, against the memory of the painting that utterly outshines it, is challenging. Old Delft is celebrated for its state of preservation, and it is almost perfectly preserved, except for the outermost walls on this end, the brick-and-limestone ramparts, gates, and towers from the Golden Age; in other words, except for nearly everything depicted in Vermeer's painting. An apartment building or two, built in the 1960s, dominate the left-hand side of the vista (Kaldenbach had warned me, rather dejectedly, about this). As for the steeples, the Oude Kerk is now barely visible; the Nieuwe Kerk is dingy with age, but is still imposing. To the right of the bridge, where the main Delft canal enters the Kolk, there is a white storefront with signs reading "CartridgeWorld." Buses, houseboats, opportunistic gulls.

I wander along a long, narrow canal around the Kolk. But before I enter the city, I glance back toward Vermeer's standpoint on the other side. The day is just beginning. Two of the girls (I recognize an orange bikini, pink bikini), one after the other, dive soundlessly into the leaden waters. Their white feet flash into the little salvoes they make, like the feet in Bruegel the Elder's *Icarus*. If I'd thought to ask their names, I could have put them here.

6. A Grave

Then I turn and lose myself almost immediately in bystreets and bridges, aiming for the Markt and the site of Maria Thins' house, the last Vermeer residence and his principal studio (Maria Thins was the mother of Vermeer's wife, Catharina). It's mostly wrong turns, of course. In the mid-morning lull, I take a seat in a café directly behind the Nieuwe Kerk. The proprietress stands chatting in Dutch for a while before she notes my blank smile and says, "You fooled me," as she points toward the hometown newspaper unfolded before me. (I'm only looking at the pictures.) "Looking for Vermeer," I say. She nods vaguely over there, *over there*, and sets down my café au lait.

A little while later, I'm staring at a plaque on a corner in Oude Langendijk, right off the Markt, that marks the site of the Vermeer house. The plaque is the work of Dr. Kaldenbach:

> The home of Delft artist Johannes Vermeer (1632–1675) once stood on this corner. He lived here in "Papenhoek," the Catholic quarter, with his wife, Catharina Bolnes. In his first-floor studio on the street side of the building, Vermeer painted his famous cityscapes and interiors filled with magical light. . . .

Today, the sprawling, nineteenth-century Maria van Jesse Catholic Church occupies the block of the Oude Langendijk where Maria Thins' house once stood. The actual space of the Vermeer home is now taken up by a very small side-chapel with its own, tiny entrance off an alley. No one's inside when I go in and sit. The pews face north, the left side is outer wall, the right a barred entrance to the main nave, where the pews face the other way. Because of its location, here in the Papenhoek, where Mass had to be held in secret, I see the luminous little chapel as a sort of memorial. And it's a lovely place, which Kaldenbach had described as "hallowed ground." Yet I feel nothing.

What had I expected? The cast of north light filtering down from the left as in the paintings, stray sounds of the Markt, stillness of the hours? It is, but it isn't here. The chapel, belonging to another age, has nothing to do with Vermeer. It isn't his space anymore. I realize immediately that this is how it should be. I swallow, pause for a moment, then turn to go.

Abruptly the Nieuwe Kerk carillon begins to chime, shivering through the modern stained glass. I can't place the song, some sort of country waltz. Then I remember that the bells were replaced the year Vermeer was painting *View of Delft*. These are the same bells he would've heard—reverberating through every square inch of his studio—for most of his working life. So I listen and listen and wait for the carillon to end before taking my leave, out through the side entrance, back toward the Markt again.

My next stop is but a couple of dozen yards away: the Nieuwe Kerk itself. It is a high, bright sanctuary, dominated by William of Orange's ornate marble mausoleum, placed where I might expect an altar. This Dutch landmark (the architect was Hendrick De Keyser, who also designed Amsterdam's beloved Westerkerk) is probably the grandest monument in the entire country, always a mainstay of the tour circuit. Painters came for inspiration and beggars worked the area for easy pickings even in Vermeer's day. It's an operatic, canopied deathbed effigy complete with weeping cherubs, a likeness of the beloved hero's dog, and the memento mori of grinning skulls. Which gives me a faint case of the creeps.

The Markt happens to be a market this particular day, and I wind my way very slowly through the rows of fragrant fish stalls, cheese stalls. The steeple chimes the hour again, but the pigeons milling about the square—wherever they find a few square feet—don't fly away or even stir.

I walk circuitously toward the leaning tower of the Oude Kerk, visible over a bank or two of rooftops. The older, brick and white stone church, like the newer one, was originally Catholic, but was stripped bare by iconoclasts during the Reformation. Walking into it, it feels unfinished, undecided, and in fact, its gothic cruciform shape was never completed. There's only part of one of the crossing halls, the northern one. I walk on the foot-worn markers, tour the entire space—without finding any trace of Vermeer at all—then go back to the entrance, and purchase a guide map in the souvenir shop.

Vermeer's grave is located a bit off center, where the crossing would have been. There's only the chiseled name and dates on a stone perhaps sixteen inches square: an ordinary stone in the floor. I stare at it balefully. Suddenly I don't know why I'm here. My visit to Delft is over.

I resign myself to wandering aimlessly. I buy a big, conical purple candle for Sophia, because it's goofy and sparkly and I know she will love it. For myself, I buy a small Delft porcelain plate, painted a rich ultramarine, because it looks authentic—it looks like Delft. It depicts a long-tailed bird, maybe a pheasant.

Eventually, late afternoon, I stumble onto the tourist information office in the center of the city. The girl at the desk is probably a university student, twenty or twenty-one. Thin, brunette, thick glasses, reading a fat paperback novel I can't make out. I say I'm looking for Vermeer. She fishes for a brochure beneath the counter, but stops, mid-gesture, and looks at me again, a conspiratorial look in her great dark eyes.

"There's nothing left," she confides.

"I know," I say. "But I've come a long way."

"Sorry," she says, with a little smile. She opens a map and points at the standpoint for *View of Delft*.

"You can still go there," she says. "But it looks nothing like it did then."

"I know. I was there."

She brightens. "If you want to see what it looked like in Vermeer's day, go to the Oostpoort." She traces a route with a slender thumb along the Oosteinde canal to, and through, the city's last remaining gate. She also makes a little X on my map just past the Oostpoort, in the Oostplein, site of a great ice-cream shop. "Do you like ice cream?"

I don't say anything, but nod so emphatically she has to smile, the afternoon sun lighting her pale, freckled face—her luminous teeth—and says she often stops there when she goes to the Oostpoort.

Walking out through the northeast quarter of town, I pass a *kleuterschool* (preschool), a library, a laundromat, a bike repair shop. Sophia will later point out, looking at a digital photo, that the Oostpoort looks like a small castle—with two very slender round brick towers on either side of the entrance, each pierced with arrow slits. In front of all this, there's a lovely water gate with a drawbridge, for the Oostpoort secured the road as well as the canal. There were once eight similarly fortified gates in the royal city. A ragged remnant of wall, about two feet long, is still attached to either side of the Oostpoort.

In the ice cream shop, I order "bosbessen," because it's the only word on the menu I believe I can pronounce. Surprisingly, the girl—with a slight smile—repeats it back with exactly the same pronunciation. It's an exquisite flavor of bilberry, as it turns out, the best in Holland, for seventy euro-cents. By the time I wander back to the station on the other side of the city's heart, the market is dismantled—all but the lingering odor of herring, the fumes of delivery trucks—and the cafés are filling up, the bikes all clattering home.

7. A Poem

I don't know what I'd expected from Delft—to see the city in the painting or the painting in the city. But as I wandered the streets full of tourists and students, I imagined what I did not see: glazed tiles, Persian carpets, maps, blue leather chairs, the plaster wall. And I imagined Vermeer's studio—what it must have meant, that paradise of hours. The artist's dream, I think, is simply to vanish into his vision. Keats and his nightingale, Vermeer and his studio.

Later, I'm left with doubt—as if I've struck a complete blank—but I'm also left with a Marble notebook filled with scribblings. One night, wondering what to make of my notes, I draft a poem called "View of Delft," using some of the better images. At once I realize I'll be writing more poems. This one ends:

> . . . No matter how
> decisively the pointillés describe
>
> seams in the stone, the scene—no matter how
> invitingly sun warms the unseen center—
>
> what I'm left with, looking back upon
> this hour, this loveliness, remains a distance
>
> I can't cross, a city I can't enter.

ANNE

[November]

It's Friday afternoon. I'm traipsing about a vast and sodden lawn—trying to keep my Rockports dry—looking for the entrance to a sprawling, former high school in the Piedmont. Now it's a luxury condo redevelopment called "The Varsity." I'm here to meet the owner/renovator of the place, a recently retired school principal close to my age. "The Varsity," apparently, wasn't the school where she had worked; she had inherited it when her father passed, and it had been closed for a number of years before she redeveloped it. All of this seems unnecessarily confusing.

This is my first Match.com date. I've done it—the whole computer dating thing—a little skeptically, with my counselor Tracy's gentle coaxing. When I sign up, I'm prompted for a username, and draw a blank, and because I don't really care, I take one of the silly suggestions: "Ariesguy24." (Thereafter, for months, I field numerous questions about the personal significance of this tag. Am I twenty-four? Believe in astrology? No and no.) I begin winnowing pages of ads, the flattering snapshots of smiling, cup-half-full women sitting at bars, proffering a toast—or leaning, windblown, against the rail of a sailboat or beach cottage—in fifteen or twenty minutes. (It's really odd, I just want to say, how many women claim to love NASCAR, football, and Harleys.) There's a giddy, kid-in-the-candy-store feeling to all the winks and IM's . . . but it fades pretty fast.

I skim the ads when I come home from work—three heads to a row, six rows to a page—each night's catch of faces. I set up coffees, lunches, beach walks. More than once I can't recognize them when I see them (though the photos are all within the past year). Of course I smile, when I meet them, anyway.

But then I begin to hone in on Anne, and we email back and forth all October, about teaching and inspiration and burnout. Her messages come very quickly and thoughtfully. I look at one particular snapshot of her often: she's wearing jeans, standing in front of a blackboard. There's another of her skydiving; another of her in a swimsuit, with dark, bobbed hair and a killer smile; another of an abstract, mostly purple acrylic painting of hers. She's cut-to-the-chase, completely grown-up. Seems perfect.

Therefore, I make a cross-state drive on a Friday afternoon, just after one of those drenching, late fall rains. I can't shake a vaguely fugitive feeling as I circle the building, trying every locked door. At this point in my life, I've somehow not yet owned a cell phone. But I manage to blunder my way inside anyway, past the security system, up a delivery ramp. The dock is open because there's a young couple moving in, unloading their sofa out of a U-Haul truck. I locate the service elevator, exit on the sixth floor, and there, at the end of the hall is the penthouse suite. When I knock, Anne says, "Come on in," but by then, the door has already swung open. All at once, I'm standing in the middle of an enormous, luminous space, listening as she talks about the ongoing renovations, the adjoining restaurant, the nightclub, the gallery, as she puts on purple hoop earrings, adjusts the music, boils water for tea.

"How do you take it?" she says. I'm not picky.

Finally, I get to look at her. Here is the killer smile in the flesh, the flawless, uniform teeth. She's slim in her jeans, with bright green eyes and fine freckles. I love how she's let her hair go peppery gray.

The size of the room astounds, the height of the cathedral ceiling astounds, the abundance of clear north light astounds. I go to the casements, holding a cup I suspect she has glazed herself. I douse the teabag up and down, releasing its jasmine fragrance, and look across the still-wet suburbs—unawakened, blonde as straw—and into the scrubbed pale skies beyond. When I look down, I notice, next to my hand, the original, articulated, brass hand-crank that swings the window out—I wonder where the bolted-down pencil-sharpener could be. Also here, on the sill, stands a cut-glass pitcher, filled to the gills with a bouquet of bright purple pinwheels. "Ninety-nine cents apiece," she says, from across the room. "I love Walmart."

She takes me up a stairway spilling down through the center of the apartment, and shows me the immaculate suite-within-a-suite where I'll be staying the night, with its enormous, claw-foot tub. It's a little odd to be spending the night on a first date, but this was her idea; it's a long drive. On our way out to tour the buildings, she opens a door on the far side of the main room, opening on whiteness, emptiness, and the mirror twin to the space where she lives.

"I haven't decided what to do with this. Everyone tells me I should use it as a painting studio . . . But I don't paint any more. *This* is my art now," she says, gesturing around and above. She closes the door gently, as if on a sleeping ghost.

I follow her around to see the lobby, the pool, the gym, and here or there, she points out strategically preserved vestiges of the former school. For instance, she leads me down a long, strangely angled corridor full of apartments. Over the doorway at the end is a fragment of the old proscenium arch—complete with the original plaster comedy-and-tragedy masks—that would have crowned the peak of the "fourth wall." The rest has been filled in with sheetrock and carpeting and elevators.

"*Oklahoma*," I say, half-singing the syllables.

She smiles once more, a sudden flash. "*Saturday Night Fever*, more likely."

"Ha, you're right," I say.

Flash-forward a couple of hours, past the delicate "nouvelle" dinner (some sort of medallions, in some sort of sauce, with pale stalks of asparagus) in her restaurant, where the music—an excellent Blue Ridge folk duet—is too loud for relaxed conversation. I'm never quite comfortable, my back to the light, my elbows constantly in the path of the waitresses.

We're back at her place again. I'm sitting on a velvety black sofa. She's boiling water again, more a formality than anything else. I become conscious, with a sudden chill, there are virtually no books in her house. Yet on the wall before me is a full-scale reproduction of one of Georgia O'Keeffe's paintings—the two pristine white calla lilies, each with its fingerlike yellow spadix, on a bright pink ground.

"It's my favorite painting," she says, setting down my cup on the end table, along with a dish of enormous, buttery, oatmeal-raisin cookies.

"I love it, too," I say.

"I have it on my back."

"You what?"

"Tattooed. On my back. That painting."

I nibble a cookie for a moment. "Curiouser and curiouser," I say . . . "May I see it?"

"Sure," she says. She turns without rising from the sofa, unbuttons her long-sleeved white shirt, slips out of it, and then, in a moment, reaches back to unclasp her black bra, and slips that off her shoulders as well. She remains sitting; back sinuously turned toward me, arms lightly crossed, unashamedly, over her small breasts.

It isn't a detail from the canvas, but the canvas itself—the vertical rectangle, reduced in size to cover the field of her back. There is a heightened vividness to the colors—white and yellow and green and pink—as a result of being translated from oil to needle-and-ink, and it is impressive, if unsettling.

"Wow," I say.

"I don't regret it," she says. She stands, slips the shirt back on without the bra, and buttons it halfway up.

She opens up, in a rush, it seems, about the period after her divorce. Her father's death that same year. How she'd inherited the corporation, and had had a crisis, partly because she didn't really want to retire from teaching. And yet, she wasn't teaching at the time—and the demands of being principal had been too stressful, anyway. She tells me how she'd done it, taken the property on, out of the blue, as an experiment, as part of a slew of midlife changes, and had discovered she liked it, had a knack for it—her head filled with a million projects, every day, these days. The vision, then the satisfaction of seeing the actual results. And the skydiving, the tattoo. "These things are a part of me now." Still, it's her dream to get back to the classroom someday, she says. And she will, she says.

My own changes seem comparatively simple, partly because I leave out the agony of my divorce. I tell her only about my joys: the hours with my daughter (I show her my wallet photos). Looking at Vermeer. And my own love of teaching, which I can't foresee leaving. Ever. This is something we share.

It's late. Hours must have passed. She offers me a firm, goodnight hug—a moment, a genuine moment of warmth.

After she retires, I take a long, luxurious bath in the claw-foot tub. I float, I drift, my legs stretched out in the almost-scalding water. What an odd song, I think. This evening, this meeting, had not been what I'd hoped for, not what I would have chosen for myself, but it was lovely in its own gentle way.

Next morning, Anne has an early meeting with contractors. At 7:45, I draw the door shut behind me. After I pull out onto the street, I stop at a Kwik-Mart, just down the hill. While the car is filling up, I grab a large, bad coffee, with an Otis Spunkmeyer blueberry muffin. Thus armed, I drive five hours back across the state.

The broad-crowned pines become a solid wall as the road levels out on the coastal plain.

When I get home, there's an email from Anne. How much she had enjoyed our night, hearing about my daughter, talking about art. Next time, it will be her turn, she promises, to make the drive.

I write back, *It was my pleasure.* Then I sketch out my schedule over the next few weeks for her. I tell how amazing she is, how much I want to see her again. That's what I say.

But no one makes the drive, and she never writes again.

WASHINGTON, D. C.

[December]

1. The Studio

I'm walking through the peculiarly cold, damp air of Washington, D. C., on a rainy winter morning, December 26. My car is parked a few blocks from the Mall. Christmas had quietly passed, my holiday ending when I dropped Sophia off at her mom's new townhouse, promptly at two on Christmas afternoon. A pall of sentimental wood smoke hung on the gray air. This year, the new, younger husband, Hans, answered the door and let Sophia in. His smile was raw and cautious, and he didn't know whether to try to shake my hand. I half-raised my own hand, as if to wave, then backed away.

These are miserable moments. Anyone can see that he is a better match for Sara than I ever was. It's the aftermath of the divorce, with little relief in the feeling of defeat.

I've driven seven hours to see *Woman Holding a Balance*.

I've been to Washington before. In fact I was born here, in 1956, when my dad was teaching for a year at Georgetown, and I've been back many times. No matter: in the same way a painting becomes something else when you come to it in need, so cities can come alive for us and reveal their hidden worlds. But not this one, not today.

Now that I'm middle-aged, I think sometimes of Donald Justice's poem "Men at Forty." It begins:

> Men at forty
> Learn to close softly
> The doors to rooms they will not be
> Coming back to.

"The doors to rooms they will not be / Coming back to," I think, as I walk down Pennsylvania Avenue. I linger, for a moment, in front of the United States Navy Memorial. It's a plaza surrounded with an arrangement of flagpoles and patriotic, heroic bas-reliefs. I imagine it might've held more interest for me in an earlier life. Maybe when I was eighteen or nineteen, and in the Navy myself. Maybe not.

I turn toward the domed National Gallery on the Mall, and cross the street. The Cabinet Galleries within offer a permanent exhibition containing the four Vermeers, part of a Dutch suite that opened in 1995. The space was built expressly for the intimate Dutch and Flemish "cabinet paintings." The term refers to small paintings, often actually kept in cabinets, such as Pieter de Hooch's *A Dutch Courtyard,* Paulus Potter's *A Farrier's Shop,* and Adriaen van Ostade's *The Cottage Dooryard.* Vermeer comes last, in this lineage, like an exclamation mark.

But immediately on entering the museum from the ground-floor Constitution Avenue entrance, I come to a small placard signpost of Vermeer's *Girl with a Red Hat* and the words "Dutch Painting" in red. An arrow points into the sculpture gallery. The Dutch suite is on the second floor, which is the main floor, but it turns out, due to a special exhibition, a small sampling of the Dutch and Flemish paintings, including the Vermeers, is now on temporary display here.

A moment later, I once again feel the shock of stepping into a room lit by Vermeers. From left to right are *Girl with a Red Hat, Woman Holding a Balance,* and *Woman with a Flute.* The small size of these paintings is startling. *Red Hat,* painted on a wooden panel, like the similar *Flute,* is only about nine by seven inches. *Woman Holding a Balance* is one of the many Vermeers that seem much bigger than they really are. But it's about twice the size of the two tiny paintings on each side of it. These three hang crowded together in a tiny room, with a handful of other tiny Golden Age works, including Jan Philips Van Thielsen's astonishing *Rose and Tulip in a Glass Vase,* and Pieter Brueghel the Elder's *River Landscape.* The fourth Vermeer, a larger, opulent canvas called *A Woman Writing* hangs just around a corner, in the next room.

One advantage of the temporary grouping is that the room is absolutely quiet and intimate; I feel alone with the paintings, as if under glass. I stare and stare. Because *Woman Holding a Balance* is a masterpiece, because I want to start with something less majestic and work up, I ignore it at first. I fold my corduroy jacket over my arm, put on my reading glasses, and focus on *Girl with a Red Hat*.

The pull of the girl's feverish, apparitional glance seems out of proportion to its tiny size, its colors, anything definable. I'd begun to feel comfortable in Vermeer's room, the corner with cool light falling from left to right, its lovely girl, its measured quietness. But none of that holds true here, in this very different scene, and I don't know why. The immediate connection is *The Girl with a Pearl Earring*, the other passionately confrontational glance. And in fact these works, along with the *Girl with a Flute* and the *Study of a Young Woman*, in New York's Metropolitan Museum of Art, have much in common. They are sometimes considered "tronies," a Dutch genre that art critic Alejandro Vergara defines as "paintings of busts or heads, generally wearing hats or exotic clothes and depicting anonymous or fictive characters." Tronies weren't considered portraits—or even finished paintings—but demonstrations of skill for the open market.

Two or three times, then, Vermeer's magic wand was left on the shelf. Which is to say the gaze—the exquisitely calibrated practice of the studio, finely tuned as it was to strip the veil from the appearances of things—was left on the shelf in favor of a radically different method. And *we* are the unexpected subject—*we,* rather than the enchanted room, are what is seen into. The barriers the paintings erect are turned inside out, and figures like this fiery woman reach out to us passionately across the fourth wall and into our own dreams.

I'm standing before *Red Hat,* jotting my impressions in my Marble notebook. What I see is focused centrally, the red hat a curved swathe of lacerating, neon red that, on closer inspection, turns out to be composed of several graduated tints, turning at the edges to feathery brush-flecks. The girl's cloak is a sumptuous ultramarine, with patterns of white and yellow. The center of the painting is not her dark eyes—that seem actually to recede beneath the shadow of the hat—but her remarkably lush, full-lit, and full-lipped mouth. All her forwardness is projected there, surrounded by curious highlights. On each side, for instance, she's wearing enormous, hollow, glass-pearl earrings, like the exquisite, almost invisible earring in *The Girl with a Pearl Earring*. The shape is entirely implied by the vaguely comma-shaped touch of white lead that reads as reflection and contour. The ornament, the romance is nearly ghost or memory.

Beneath the chin—precisely defined along the right-hand, illumined edge, but shadow-smudged on the left—she's wearing a translucent lace scarf, nothing more than an incandescent, smoke-like swirl. Toward the left, as the scarf slips into shadow, it disappears, except for a few patches of optically-blurred white light.

The girl's lush mouth is perhaps even more provocative than the mouth of *The Girl with a Pearl Earring*, but her nose complicates things. She has been called "somewhat androgynous" by Walter Liedtke (a curator at the Metropolitan Museum of Art), and that certainly applies to her rather small eyes and long Dutch nose, which is straight-bridged, with slightly large nostrils. It's at odds with her delicate, yet arrestingly sensuous lips. Her mouth and nose are linked by a strikingly defined, sunlit cleft on the upper lip, itself part of her idiosyncratic look. Because of all these complications, it might be difficult for me to call the girl pretty, exactly, but neither does this diminish her. And I'm not off the hook. Her eyes bore into me, a moment's dead level appraisal from arm's length, over her right shoulder—just as the Mauritshuis girl glances from across her own left shoulder. The scale of both paintings puts me within inches of a face, a gaze, which sees through me completely.

But the shadowed gaze of this tiny girl gives nothing up—unlike the other's eyes, which give away all. The upper two-thirds of her face dissolves, the right ear little more than a beige semi-circle. She's wearing no makeup to bring out her eyes; and her forehead, with no visible brows or lashes, has a smooth, masklike appearance. There's an odd—radical, even—oval green highlight floating on the surface of her right eye. In all, the neutral steadiness of her dark gaze couldn't contrast more with the warmth of her passionate, flowery mouth—its glint of teeth, of tongue. I squint into the shadows, but I can't tell what she's thinking. Finally, a distinct bright pink blush fills the girl's cheeks. She is desire and acceptance and fate, rather than comfort or understanding. This is what makes the painting so troubling, yet irresistible and paradoxically consoling to me. I can't look away. Georgia O'Keeffe once said: "Nobody sees a flower, really—it is so small it takes time—we haven't time—and to see takes time, like to have a friend takes time."

After such intensity, such clawing at the heart, I puzzle over details: the strangely exotic mosaic of abstractions surrounding this particular girl. Because they are closer to us than the area in focus—which is centered on her mouth—the lion-head finials on the chair-back are a blurry jangle of reflections. The background appears as a very free, somewhat Matisse-like screen, with a calligraphic, decorative, or architectural motif. The artist's signature is a monogram above the hat, integrated into the design.

The young girl, *who* she is—the dead-level particularity of her glance—gathers willfully, unforgettably, out of a ground of indeterminacy and dream, from whose depths she herself and everything around her is composed. Because I have felt such immense longing and seen it reflected in a lover's eyes, I feel it again now in every nerve.

2. Balance

When I do pull away, I refocus on the larger work just to the right, *Woman Holding a Balance.*

There's an ethereal simplicity, a radiance surrounding this woman that feels overtly religious. She looks beatific, I think; she looks like purity incarnate. Vermeer is inside his recurring room, his dream, and he approaches the presence of this woman with utter reverence. She stands before a table scattered with pearls and gold coins and chains, delicately holding a balance between right thumb and index finger. She is checking its accuracy by weighing nothing. (Much ink has been spilled on what the balance pans contain. The painting was traditionally called *The Gold Weigher*. But it's clear, now that the work has been thoroughly cleaned, that each pan holds a small highlight of reflection and nothing else.)

Edward Snow concludes his beautiful book, *A Study of Vermeer*, with a discussion of this painting. He obsesses over the contrast between the woman's serene balance and what is depicted in the painting hanging directly behind her. It's an apocalyptic, Bosch-like Last Judgment with a seated Christ raising both arms above a writhing horde of naked sinners. Snow believes the baroque, moralizing Christian values as reflected in the wall painting are directly contradicted by the secular scene before it. He sees this triumph as the essence of Vermeer.

I crane in close to see the Last Judgment. It's a let down, though, for as close as I get, I can hardly make out *anything* in the wall painting behind the woman. I polish my glasses on a shirttail and try again. I can more or less see where Christ is, and a few flame-like shapes of the sinners beneath him, but that's about it. This might be partially due to the lighting in the small temporary space—there's either not enough of it or too much reflection off the glass and/or the painting's glaze. For whatever reason, the painting-within-the-painting is largely illegible, as such details often are in Vermeer's work.

Yet when I step back and look at the woman again, I'm as defenseless before her as I was before *The Milkmaid,* in the Rijksmuseum. My body feels weightless, almost insubstantial, just as it did then. I stand so still I have to remind myself to breathe. But the lady here is very different: small-boned, long-limbed, her heavy-lidded attention settled sweetly on her task. One of the mysteries hovering over her—as well as the Amsterdam letter-reader—involves her bell-shaped appearance. A sliver of yellow-gold blouse peeks out from her dark blue morning coat trimmed with white fur (the same jacket as in two other Vermeers), and calls attention to the noticeable swell of her midriff. It's difficult to tell if she's pregnant or if Vermeer was simply accurately portraying a Dutch fashion of the time, as some experts claim. And maybe Vermeer didn't intend her pregnancy—or anything else about her—to be read literally. There's simply no way to know. I stare at her in childish wonder.

In *The Milkmaid*, I stared at the maid's big, work-hardened left hand steadying the heavy pitcher from beneath, her wrist tanned where the mustard-yellow sleeve has been turned back. If that painting is earthen, the later *Woman Holding a Balance* is delicate, pure spirit. (This shift was true for Dutch art in general during Vermeer's life, as tastes evolved from rustic to more refined, or bourgeois, subject matter.)

I notice the softness embodied in the sunlit fingertips holding the balance, the woman's little finger extended horizontally as if to steady the gesture. The fingertips of the other hand light softly on the table's edge, so softly she seems to lend support as much as seek it. The ink-blue tablecloth is pushed roughly back, revealing not only the jewelry and gold coins lying about the naked tabletop, but the table's massive, intricately carved underpinnings as well. It's about the connection, the give and take between the darkness of the world and the woman's calming touch. Her figure is a bright star pulsing quietness into my heart.

3. Shadow Hand

There is a third hand in this painting that I can't help gazing at for a good half hour. I'll explain. The woman is wearing a linen cap or headdress, meant to protect the hairdo, like the one in *The Milkmaid*. The cap in *Woman Holding a Balance* is disturbingly crisp. The creases in the fabric about her brow look as if they would be sharp to the touch. The charcoal and umber shadow along the right side of her head is nuanced and striking. Very powerfully the shadow suddenly takes the shape of a human hand, and it's eerily well defined. Almost as if by touching them with his fingers, Vermeer works with the textures and folds of the linen, subtly coaxing form from the natural drape of the cloth, so that the hand doesn't seem contrived. I first became aware of this effect, this shadow hand, from a paragraph in Edward Snow's *Study of Vermeer*. Snow describes the hand first as a "touch of death" that later grows benign. Standing here, I see it only as helpful, caressing the left side of the woman's face, gathering all the painting's tenderness there, at once a spiritual gesture and an optical trick.

I look at the shadow, look back at the balance. The woman herself is the equipoise the balance only alludes to: her right hand effortlessly holds the scales at rest, her left hand lightly touches the table's edge. It's startling even now, as I write this, to recall the luminous, almost sculptural serenity of her face—braced by the shadow hand, and by her body's fullness, so sweetly borne.

4. The Wall

I pore over the white-washed wall. I'm especially delighted to find a trompe-l'oeil nail with a tiny shadow here, above and to the left of the maid's face. This effect seems to have been reproduced almost verbatim from *The Milkmaid*—as if to link the two great women, the two great masterpieces. But the plaster this time looks smooth to the touch, more elegant, befitting the lady's status. All around her, the delicate umber shadows spread to the corners. I wear my eyes out staring at the nuances, as though the wall were an unabridged dictionary in a tiny font.

Finally, I marvel at the ruffs on the woman's morning jacket that really are as irresistibly touchable as a painter could make them, and at the jewelry that consists mostly of carefully placed highlights on opaque dabs of paint—like the famous earring. Then I take a step backward in this room, where the teeming Dutch and Flemish still-lifes press in all around. I'm reminded that Dutch art of the Golden Age—whether portraits or still-lifes, or the genre scenes that dominated through the 1650s—tends to share one overriding concern: to "follow nature," as Rembrandt advised. And, in fact, as I slip into the next room—the one that contains *A Lady Writing*—I'm immediately drawn into the orbit of a Rembrandt. It's a portrait of his wife Saskia, from 1634. The expressiveness of details—the impossibly fine articulation of her bountiful red-gold curls, the evanescent lace at her throat—is simply beyond comparison. Similar details in Vermeer seem humble, if not willfully crude, in contrast.

What then is the source of Vermeer's authority? Why is it that Dutch schoolchildren, on viewing the trickle of milk in *The Milkmaid* for the first time, exclaim: "It really pours!"

But no one can answer such questions. I leave that room, as well, and take a random stroll through corridor after corridor of the vast collection. There are many rooms filled with busy tableaus, large-scale pictorial histories that leave me cold today. It's as if I were walking through the Gallery of the Western World, the landscapes and portraits leaning toward me on each side, the walls receding into the distance as far as the eye can see—when suddenly, the lights go out, and the hall, the great cathedral of canvases, goes dark.

And it's a long, dark walk from Vermeer to Degas, when once again the human form itself is all. The lights come on, and the eye, the lens, is open.

5. *Straight Shot*

I find a place to sit on a marble bench in the magnificent central rotunda. In the middle of it all, there's a winged statue of Mercury, towering above his fountain and temporarily surrounded by hundreds of potted Christmas poinsettias and amaryllis. I'm worn out. Certainly this bottom is something like the other one, I'm thinking. Of course, no one is ever grateful for the damages caused by a family breaking up, or the loss of control over one's life that comes with alcoholism or addiction.

But I have experienced something more this time. When I walked into the room in the Rijksmuseum in Amsterdam and the force of the Vermeers broke over me like a wave, mercy and equipoise hit dead center in a soul in serious need of them. In some profound, mysterious way, those paintings had the measure of me and of my heartbreak.

Here's the thing: Vermeer did not invent himself or the stillness and clarity of his gaze for critics and historians to mull over. More than for those who want it, the light of Vermeer is intended for those who need it. This specific purpose or reason for each work's existence not only underscores the urgency of each work, but also might help explain why there are only thirty-five Vermeers in the world: such manifestations of clarity and grace cannot have come often to him, to anyone.

Suddenly, I realize I won't always have this need, this purpose, the hunger that is spurring me on through galleries at closing time. I stand—my legs feel fresh again. I hurry back to the Vermeers to stand before them for the last half hour. This time, I leave my notebook in my backpack, which I stash in a corner with my jacket.

An executive-type in a khaki safari outfit comes into the room. He pauses briefly but decisively before each picture—as if checking off some box in his head—then moves on to the next. Finally, he stops directly in front of *Woman Holding a Balance*. I step back. He unsheathes his camera; for a moment I can see the orange dot projected by the sensor as it tracks across the canvas, settles on the woman's throat. When I look again, he's gone.

And now a guard comes forward and tells me, "Sir, the museum is closing." I put my jacket on, pull myself together. The weigher of souls, counterpart of St. Michael, is still focused on her task.

Stepping out into the diffuse, rainy air, I think of Vermeer and his eleven children. How serene his vision; how manic his life must actually have been. I remember his standing debt to the baker, Hendrick van Buyten, who received one painting while Vermeer was still living and two more from Catharina, after Vermeer's death, in settlement for the family's bread.

Then I consider the deep, uncanny solace of Vermeer's room: the gaze, the visual field in which we—whoever we are—take root for the moment. *Look: a Vermeer.* His work isn't necessarily comforting: *Girl with a Red Hat* has left me feeling burned, aspersed, my heart tricked out of its hiding place.

But I feel noticeably buoyed as I follow Pennsylvania Avenue toward the side street where my car is parked. Suddenly hungry, I wonder, Is there a good restaurant nearby? Yes. I can smell the garlic, smoke, and minted lamb from a Greek café. I follow my nose; the aroma hits me hard at the next corner.

After I feast, it's six hours south on I-95, a straight shot home.

6. *Poems*

For ten hours a day through the next few weeks, I work on poems—happily, happily—trying to capture the images while they're still fresh. I use the turns and rhythms of poetry to try to think my way into the heart of each scene. In my poem on *Woman Holding a Balance,* I write: "All we know of her is what we see: / how—weightless, effortless / as flame—she stands to face the lightfall over the umber, / oilcloth-covered table . . ." The poem ends on this note:

> It won't come again—
> this equipoise between
>
> the figure & the room. Vermeer is thirty-two—
> the death-carts creaking through
>
> the black smoke of North Europe. Twenty-four thousand dead
> in Amsterdam this year.
>
> In June, the war with England will resume. So it
> won't come again, I'm thinking,
>
> not with such full-bodied ease. But for the moment,
> here she stands. Is realized.

As the year goes on, I find I've written an entire book of poems from the Marble notebook. I call it *Vermeer in Hell.*

STEPHANIE

[March]

1. Out of My League

I'm on my way to meet Stephanie, wearing an uncomfortable, pressed shirt, when I hit town in the thick of Friday rush hour. It's March, unseasonably warm. There are two four-lane bypasses on the outskirts of the Triangle, an inner loop and an outer loop. After I trace a complete lap going clockwise, looking for an exit that never materializes, I circumnavigate halfway back again, into bright sun, on the other loop. Although Raleigh is only two hours from Wilmington, I come only about once a year, and so don't know my way. It feels like I've been toiling nowhere, in Dantesque circles, for a small eternity.

But the house, when I finally find it—by giving up, wandering off the freeway until I find a gas station with a pay phone, and calling her to get directions—couldn't be less imposing, more ordinary. It's an older white duplex, with the original metal awnings over the windows, on a quiet downhill street amok with parti-colored dogwoods and magnolias. I draw the handbrake and, stressed because I'm late, head for the door. There's a tidy flowerbed where nothing has yet bloomed (I find out later there will be tulips, which we seldom see on the coast), and the boxwoods are happy. I look down a little dubiously at the roses I'm holding, which have lain limp on the passenger seat all afternoon.

Stephanie is an attorney, six months older than I am. We've been messaging back and forth for weeks. It's my last Match.com date, I've decided; I'm feeling burnt out after only a few months. In fact, I'd already more or less quit. But my subscription hadn't quite run out; Stephanie had seen my ad, and despite the distance, she'd winked, she'd written, she'd been the aggressor. It's *her* last Match date as well, she says. One last shot. She wants to see how this works out, but then, she's done, she says. It's not for her, either.

Stephanie is not the sort of date a guy, this guy anyway, turns down.

What I'd liked about her profile: a somber, sober photo of a slender blond in a black shirt, not trying too hard. Her "exercise habits": *daily*. Her "favorite things": *my job, poetry, daily meditation*. "Last read": *legal briefs, Dylan Thomas, As Bill Sees It, your ad*.

Because of the reference to *As Bill Sees It*, I knew she was also in recovery, and this promise of a kindred spirit was the most attractive thing about her. When I'd googled her, I'd found a photo of her entire law firm: no one smiling, standing like soldiers in glossy, dark-blue suits. The kind of shot designed for a billboard, back of a phone book. Sic 'em, I thought. She's in front, the team-player blonde.

I'd also found, and read, a lengthy court brief she had authored, tracing the legal history of sodomy. It's all very thorough, and I was impressed.

"You're late," she says. She's standing in the center of a seamlessly low-key, modestly out-of-style stylish living room. Everything rounded, a little deco, and earth-tone. Clean.

She's wearing iridescent, black three-quarter tights, a lavender Lycra top, and high-end Nikes. Startlingly taut and leggy, rippling unselfconsciously. Holding a bottle of Aquafina: tipping it back for a deep swig. Looking me over as she does—her eyes steel-blue, her sun-illumined hair drawn taut with a red rubber band.

This is the first Match ad I've answered where the photo doesn't do justice to the person. Typically, sadly but understandably, it's the other way around. In a single, clipped-short breath—I can see I'm out of my league.

"I wasn't sure you were coming," she says, with a slight smile, "so I went for a quick run. Here, let's get these into water."

She's standing over the kitchen sink, washing, stripping, and clipping the roses with shears. I notice the small, white, electric stove behind me, which looks almost identical to the one I got rid of recently. But hers looks virtually unused—even the wrinkled foil that wraps the drip pans beneath the four coils shines immaculate.

"Three red, three white, six pink," she says. Do you know what this means?"

"Means?" I say. "It means I wanted red, but they only had three left."

She brings out a glass vase from beneath the sink, and begins to arrange the stems. "In the language of flowers, red roses signify passion, romance. Pink is for admiration. White is for reverence."

"Well then," I say, "I really admire you *so far*."

She smiles, and shows me around. Her study, the spare bedroom, is simple, peaceful, well lit on two sides, and it fills me with envy. I tell her I once had a study almost exactly like this. It's now Sophia's room. I don't mind, don't miss it much. But I'm suddenly jealous.

"I want you to see something," she says. She draws out a thin, cream-colored, letter-press journal from a low bookshelf. It's her high school literary magazine. It falls open to a poem of hers. "It's probably bad," she says, "but it's a poem."

I look it over: it's a slender, 1970s-style, free-verse lyric called "Thistle." Competent, I think. "Hey, I like it," I say.

2. Handbook

Five minutes later, she emerges from her bedroom, showered and changed into jeans and an ivory top. I'm standing in her living room, staring at the hulk of an antique radio that has been charred black—the humpbacked kind with two dials and a mesh sound hole.

"I used to collect those," she says. "I went to auctions and flea markets, all my life. I had over fifty, if you can believe it. Two years ago I lost my house in a fire. I keep this one because it was all I was able to save."

I stand quietly for a minute. "I'm not upset about it," she adds. "It forced me into recovery."

"You went out with a bang."

"Yeah," she says.

She says she'll drive. "You ready?"

Outside, the door of her immaculate white BMW coupe shuts with a thud, and we buckle up in black leather. "Sometimes, I feel like my father driving this big *thang*," she says, "I always drove Miatas or motorcycles. That's the real me."

Pulling away, she nails it, with a stab of her foot. Thrown back as the rear wheels chirp, I grab the door handle, half wondering if this is a joke—but she nails it again, at every stop, as if to prove her point.

On the freeway on-ramp, she pins my head back sideways—cheek pressed into the headrest—the silky V-8's snarl uncorked, and effortlessly blowing past everything in our path. Just as abruptly then, we level off around eighty. I realize we're loping along on the same freeway where I'd been wandering lost, an hour or so ago.

"You must get lots of tickets," I say, adding hastily: "I mean, *I* do. I get lots of tickets. *Unfortunately.*"

"You should read the Driver's Handbook," she murmurs. Swerving right for an off-ramp, she rips off a fluid heel-toe downshift, her left foot dabbing the clutch as her right hand bats the shifter into place. We wind down quickly to the posted speed.

I glance sideways at her face to see if she's smiling, but she's watching the road.

3. Tiramisu

She is honored at her favorite restaurant in all the familiar ways. Giovanni takes time out from his pasta press, I presume, to wait, to welcome, to chat her up. Her favorite table, in the sunset window, is cleared at the nod of his head for her. I would do the same, I would feel the same, if I had a checkered tablecloth, a bentwood chair I could scoot for her, a linen napkin I could pop in the air with a snap of the wrist, a snap of the wrist, like that, for her.

A cloth-covered basket of steaming focaccia appears without request or fanfare; then shaved prosciutto with melon balls and toasted pine nuts. Giovanni appears again; he flicks a wooden match on a thumbnail, and lights the candle between us. Disappears again. He knows better than to bring the wine list.

We're just getting comfortable.

"Do you remember the Four Horsemen in the Big Book?" she asks. The sun is in my eyes, dusk guttering behind her, haloing her sleek, golden head. She picks with the tiny fork, lifts a sliver of lucent ham to her lips—the sun igniting that, too.

"Terror, Bewilderment . . ." I say.

I was a classic, low-bottom drunk, I tell her. I mean the usual peaks and valleys, helplessness, the plummeting downward spiral of blackouts and tail of the dog. Getting evicted, everything I owned—my furniture, misshapen and brown—put out on the street by a deputy with an order one afternoon. I wonder who that crap belonged to, I thought, happening to pass by the heap of my former possessions on my way to the pool hall.

"Frustration and Despair," she replies. "That whole cycle, hitting bottom . . ." She tells me about failing the bar twice, falling back on her looks, taking up with much older men—"the buck with the biggest antlers" as she puts it—for protection. Then the divorce: the months of blackout, the fire, disgrace. What it felt like, bottoming out in suburbia, as "the chilling vapor that is loneliness settled down" (as she quotes again from the Big Book). She plops another cantaloupe ball into her startling mouth.

"I remember it well. That's the part where they talk about seeking out 'sordid places,'" I venture.

I mention the hotel bar and pool hall of my last few drinking years, most of the clientele like the walking dead—which anyone could see, at a glance, except me. We were the last stop, last watch—shivering, happy-hour dead-enders, going down with the ship.

"What turned *you* around?" she asks.

I tell her about the arrests that year, mostly for idiotic bar-room brawls, assault, resisting arrest, public intoxication, destruction of property, and so forth. Then the inevitable probation officer—whom I termed a "Nazi bitch." In all fairness, even the cops didn't like her, thought she was way too tough, according to my brother Ben, a lifelong police officer with the Columbia Police Department. One day, making my afternoon call, she suspected I wasn't sober, and ordered me to come in immediately. The moment I showed up, she administered the breathalyzer, took a urine sample, then sent me off in a patrol car to lock-up for probation violation. After nine days, she came to visit. We sat at a steel table in a small, cinder-block interview room. She spread some papers between us, and asked me, smiling, whether I'd like to commit myself to treatment in state hospital, or rot where I was. And then, when I hesitated and fell silent, she gathered her papers quickly and rose without a word. I remember simply saying, "Wait," as she turned to leave. She didn't. Another five days passed on the concrete. When she came back, she asked the same question again, in the same flat tone of voice. Her smile was gone; I could tell it was my last chance. "Where do I sign?" I asked.

"I really admire people like that," Stephanie says. "We need them. Did you ever thank her?"

"Yes, as a matter of fact, I did. One day I ran into her downtown, on Ninth and Broadway. It was springtime. I was sober almost a year, and headed to graduate school. I went up to her, and thanked her. To her face. But I still hated her."

Stephanie smiles a wan smile. "But you're grateful now."

I think back, for a moment, on that first year in Alcoholics Anonymous, a quarter of a century ago. One of the most bizarre and incomprehensible terms I encountered floating about the rooms was "gratitude." For I'd known only misery as long as I could remember; I wasn't grateful for anything. Yet I kept running into recovering drunks, like myself, who were eager to identify themselves as "grateful alcoholics." My home group was even the "Gratitude Group." (I didn't realize then that there are thousands of groups with that name around the world.) The First Part of the Big Book ends with the statement: "In return for a bottle and hangover, we have been given the Keys of the Kingdom." It seemed perverse to me then, this crew of ravaged outcasts expressing gratitude for our affliction.

All that year, I worked at putting my program first. I worked the Steps with my first sponsor, Gene. He was wonderfully gruff and old-school, a professor of entomology who spent most of his time outside, in the fields, and looked it. One of the first things he did was teach me to pray. After that, I whispered the Serenity Prayer obsessively to myself, wherever I happened to be. In meetings, I learned to listen, especially to the quavering voices of the newcomers. One of my greatest fears was forgetting my own bottom—for then, I was pretty sure, I'd be doomed to repeat it. All that year, I washed dishes full-time during the day. At night, I rode to meetings in the back of Gene's truck. I could hardly stand such happiness.

I nod at Stephanie. "I'm grateful now."

Two heaping plates of Sicilian mussels arrive—steaming, and snapping fresh, with olives and capers, ladled over linguine. I twirl a bite, and chew. For all the over-the-top dive atmosphere—the bustled curtains, tri-colored wallpaper, the framed prints of Naples, Pisa, and Capri—the food is as close to real as I've had outside of Italy.

I put my fork down. *Turn the corner, give it a try*, I think. *Just lay it out there. Tell her everything.*

I look full into her eyes—it isn't easy—and I tell her how I met my first wife, Jackie, in Colorado, while I was fixing her toilet, in fact. I was a maintenance man that summer, my first full summer in sobriety. I try to tell her what that passion was like—that deep can't-get-enough of her. Then I go on, tell her my whole story. It's a little like an A.A. story: what we were like, what happened, what we are like now, but it's about more than drinking. It's about love, about luck. A timeline of every significant passion I can think of along the way. I tell her about Jackie's cancer: two years at her side, her bravery, such an intense intimacy—almost as if we were each inside the other's body, at some great remove from the rest of the world. This was back in Columbia, Missouri, where we were both from, in those last months of hospice care.

How often is it we're called to really tell everything?

She wants to know what I wanted, how I changed, what do I want now, what do I have to offer? I realize I may never have an opportunity like this again. She looks straight into my eyes, and I go on through my life, my work—keeping it to the point—through my second marriage, ending with Vermeer.

"Yeah, I was going to ask about that," she says. "*The Girl with a Pearl Earring,* right?"

I look at her, and look away. I wonder if she really wants to know about the hours in the galleries: the intense gaze that only begins to unravel what is there? But I try. I tell her about the Rijksmuseum, how I felt my knees buckle the first time I saw *The Milkmaid.* Another sort of conversion.

She listens intently. Later, she says, "I might as well tell you. I'm slow—I don't kiss anyone till I've known him at least six months," she says. "I have a trust issue."

"Pretty hard to find someone who doesn't."

"I mean, I have good reason."

She tells me about her one romance in sobriety. A law partner who split his time between a firm up north and the Raleigh office. A boyish marathon runner, a charmer. I'm getting a pretty clear picture. He was sober, too. It turned out that he talked a good game, and was clearly a great and ambitious attorney. She fell hard for him.

One day, she borrowed his cell phone, accidentally hit redial, a woman answered. That old story: Who's this? *His fiancée.* That can't be. *I'm his girlfriend.* Click.

But Stephanie went up north herself, to Philadelphia, found the other girl, and talked her into going for coffee. They got along. The other girl told her she'd been to his condo in Raleigh many times. Every other weekend, in fact. How could that be? They compare notes about the bedroom—*her* photo on the nightstand, on the dresser. It seems he changed the photos every weekend for two years—also the linen, the placemats, the vases, and of course, the toothbrush and cup in the bathroom.

"Well you know what they say," I say. "What have you got when you sober up a horse thief?"

"A sober horse thief." She nods, straight-faced.

So Stephanie has a trust issue. "I'm really sorry to hear that," I say. "That's awful."

"Anyway," she says, "my work is my love life now."

She tells me about an eighteen-year-old client of hers who is facing life. "He didn't do it," she says.

"You're sure?" I say.

"He didn't do it. His problem is, he doesn't understand how much trouble he's in. It's my job to make him understand. That's how I spend my Saturdays."

I think about this, a little amazed. I realize I have some prejudices about her profession.

"Really," I ask, "you feel that way about the law?"

"It's the matrix," she says. "It's what holds us together." Then she adds, "I've been trying, though. At romance. You wouldn't believe the dates I've had."

"Yeah, I would."

"I'm going to write a book about it," she says. "A tell-all about Match.com. I mean, after this. Depending on what happens."

We're contemplating tiramisu. "I've never even ordered it in the States," I say. "I always wanted to keep my memories pure."

"Order it here," she says. So I do.

I notice we're the last ones left. I had paid no attention as the restaurant was slowly filling—each table set and cleared and set and cleared, a handful of customers waiting in front more or less continuously—then gradually emptied again, the bentwood chairs turned upside down on the tables all around. The place is a tomb, our candlewick about to drown in a pool of wax.

"It's fabulous," I say. "I can't believe it. As good as Florence."

"It's the mascarpone," she says. "It has to be fresh."

"Tell me, Stephanie," I say. "How is it—this—working out? Because I'd like to see you again."

"Sure," she says. "Listen, there's something you should know. My firm is supposed to be opening a branch in Wilmington. I'd be the obvious choice to run it. It's one of the reasons I winked at you."

4. Keyhole

We're roaring back through the blue night. Again and again, she brakes unnecessarily hard, it seems to me, nearly pitching me into the dash. "Look," she says, glancing up toward a yellow light, after one of these stops. "See that?"

"Yeah, I see it," I say, sunk low in the seat.

"But do you know what it means?" she asks.

The instant red turns to green, her right foot pins me back in the big leather seat again.

"*Slow down*," I say. "It means, *caution, slow down.*"

"Wrong," she says. "It means: *clear the intersection*. No wonder you get tickets."

"You're right," I say. "I should read the Handbook."

When we reach her house, it's late, so I sign off in her drive. Quickly, to make it easy for her.

"I'll come to the coast in a week or two. As soon as I know something," she says.

"I'll show you around, anyway," I say, "whatever happens."

She gives me a half-hug; I can feel the long muscles in her supple, feline shoulders. I don't expect more, don't even want more. I'm happy.

Perfectly happy, driving down I-40—on my left, a half-moon, white as candle wax, rising behind the flowery crowns of the long-leaf pines. A dream, I think.

I have a chance, I tell myself. It's all I could ask for.

I write her in the morning. "No matter what," I say. "Just let me know. I'll come to you. I dreamt last night that we both bought motorcycles. We were roaring off to the mountains in the summer. Maybe a picnic, or just talking for hours beneath a waterfall. I know exactly where to go."

She writes back immediately; tells me I'm sweet. Thanks me for coming. She has a big trial coming up, she's under a lot of pressure, but she'll write again soon.

But she doesn't write back that week or the next.

Night after night, I want to email her, but decide to restrain myself.

She said she'll write, I think.

But she doesn't, she simply *doesn't*, and that's the end of it.

I'm through. Part of me thinks: two roads diverged, etcetera.

But the simple truth is that I've already gotten more from my travels—from Vermeer—than from anything else in this passage of my life. Not long ago, it seemed his art was a dream, a mirror reflecting life, or a keyhole through which we peer at it. I realize Vermeer is what's real for me now; life is the dream.

New York

[April]

1. The Gaze

Coming out of the Hunter College subway station on Lexington Avenue, I head by instinct toward Central Park a couple of blocks away. I think about the primal sense—translated from forest to city—that divines a half-seen clearing, river or open air. Even if I can't see the park, I can feel it—*there* at the end of *this* street, but not *that* one. Of course, this feeling is especially powerful in New York, with its more dramatic skyline contrasted with dramatic openness in the middle. I follow East Seventieth Street toward the April-green haze at the end of it, and arrive at the black, wrought-iron gates of the Frick Collection, on Fifth Avenue just across from the park.

The Frick and the Mauritshuis are close relatives, not only in terms of the physical buildings (former mansions), but also in terms of the feeling of intimacy and the personal eclecticism of each collection. The Mauritshuis, a nationalized seventeenth-century palace, was built by Count Johan Maurits, once governor of the Dutch colony in Brazil. Prince William V of Nassau-Orange (1748–1806) owned the original collection of Dutch and Flemish art. In 1816, his son, King William I (1772–1843), donated it to the Dutch state. The Frick, on the other hand, was the idyll, refuge, and passion of one man. It was built by the infamous Pittsburgh tycoon Henry Clay Frick, in 1913, to accommodate his personal collection of paintings and other art objects. When he died in 1919, he left the building, including all the furnishings and art, with an endowment, and so The Frick Collection was born.

Both buildings were residences—palatial, but lived-in residences, which makes them ideal for experiencing a Vermeer. The hot, seventeenth-century, Dutch art market, driven by a newly wealthy middle class buying up paintings for fashionable homes (when they weren't investing in tulips), was domestic and secular in nature. Smaller paintings, especially portraits or exotic still-lifes—filled with the luxury items a maritime economy could provide—were in. The idea of seeing a real Vermeer in somebody's living room boggles the mind nowadays, but that's the right setting for this artist's eye-level interiors, and the Frick or the Mauritshuis is as close as one gets to that experience.

The first painting I see in the Frick, in the passageway called the South Hall, is a small, jewel-like Vermeer: *Officer with Laughing Girl* (c. 1655–60). Kees Kaldenbach had called this painting "extraordinarily luminous," and it's clear, as soon as I turn the corner, why he'd said that. In this early genre piece, Vermeer imagines a relationship between the officer and the young woman that not only reflects light but, like most of the Vermeers I've seen, this one actually seems to glow. The seemingly casual placement—in a murky passageway, among period marble and velvet furnishings—only emphasizes its alchemical radiance.

Officer with Laughing Girl seems especially vulnerable, too, hanging alone and so close to the museum's outer doors, and this vulnerability is heightened by the fact that none of the paintings here are covered with glass.

I give *Officer with Laughing Girl* a wide berth at first. I linger in its vicinity. Passers-by on their way to the great galleries at the end of the hall, filled with big canvases by Rembrandt, El Greco, Velazquez, say, "Look! A Vermeer!" Just as in all the other museums. But when we're alone again, I zoom in. To do this, I have to lean over a gilt-painted antique chair, placed directly beneath the painting. A gold, tasseled rope is laid across its gold satin cushion, embroidered with cupids and bizarre, winged busts—in order to keep onlookers back, I suppose. It doesn't completely work, in my case. The gorgeousness of the painting prompts me to lean precariously over the chair, until I trigger the motion sensor. I've done this often enough, in other museums, to feel only a little shame when the alarm beeps. A smiling young guard with tight cornrows—wearing a maroon jacket like a Shriner—appears discreetly to my left. We exchange nods as I back off.

Again and again, when I glance up, my breath catches in my throat. The feeling isn't *Here is art*, but *Here is life*.

As critics point out, *Officer with Laughing Girl* comes directly (much more directly than Vermeer's later work) out of the mid-century genre tradition. It bears a striking resemblance especially to Pieter De Hooch's *The Card Players*. Vermeer painted only a few such scenes, and these early works culminate in *Officer with Laughing Girl*. Edward Snow says this painting has "the feeling more of a last than a first work." In fact it *was* a last work of sorts, as, after this, Vermeer settled almost completely on the solitary subject, his calling all along. Snow spends the middle portion of his book thinking about three further exceptions in the oeuvre, *The Concert, Couple Standing at a Virginal,* and *An Artist in His Studio,* all depictions of groups or couples. He calls these paintings "reflections on the matrix within which his solitary women take shape."

The window at left in *Officer with Laughing Girl,* especially the sun-infused lozenges of panes on the upper row, is among my favorites of all his magnificent windows. (My very favorite is the one in *The Milkmaid*.) The outside surfaces of the partially open, inward opening, right-hand casement shimmer with swirling, gray-green, platinum shapes as the light rakes over it, registering nuances as slight as the varying thicknesses of the faceted panes. Smudges, imperfections are passionately captured with Vermeer's characteristic brew of verisimilitude and freedom. On the other, still-closed casement— blue in the center, gold on the sides—I make out the ochre ghost of a building in the lower left-hand corner. Once through the window, the otherworldly flow of north light is registered by one of Vermeer's first bare walls, and is caught especially in the face of the bonneted girl.

At first I see this as a traditional genre scene, which might be taken either as a girl visiting with her suitor in her house or as a woman in a bordello "entertaining" an officer in uniform. The male figure is viewed from the back. We cannot quite see his expression as he sits across from her at a table, but he wears a bright red jacket with a sash or shoulder strap, and a large black hat, tilted jauntily. Foregrounded as he is, he's a disproportionately massive and shadowy shape. He looms between window and woman, taking up all the space and blocking the painting's left center. It's a radical perspective that suggests the use of a camera.

She, on the other hand, seems tiny, almost childlike, and emotionally open. Besides the cotton bonnet drawn closely about her face, she wears the yellow bodice with black braiding (perhaps Vermeer's most characteristic outfit), and a white collar. There's nothing overtly disclosed here to make me think of the women who appear in the traditional bawdy genre scenes of the time.

In fact, I'm deeply moved by the ways Vermeer shelters her, even from my own intense gaze. Rather than present her in the typical attire of tousled, open blouse with dramatic décolletage, he covers almost every square inch of her with the stiff, embroidered dress—only a hint of throat exposed—her bonnet tied tightly beneath her chin.

The artist Jonathan Janson, on his website *The Essential Vermeer*, summarizes critical sentiment: "It is impossible for us to ignore the young woman's radiant optimism . . . Her expression is so positively charged that even the officer's reticence is effectively dissimulated." This is what I expected to see in the Frick: another of Vermeer's serene, angelic studies like *The Milkmaid* or *Woman Holding a Balance*. The *real* Vermeer, for me.

Yet, as I keep studying her, the girl's animated presence takes me by surprise. She sits leaning a little toward the officer, hands before her on the table—her right hand lightly curled around the stem of a full wineglass. What Janson sees as "radiant optimism" can be seen in another way: her face seems almost livid, lit with alcohol and desire.

Or else she is flushed from the chill I can feel, wafting through the open window.

Yet, her lips are full and defiantly—almost shockingly—red.

Finally, I see something more: her left hand. There's a single gesture at the heart of this painting—it's how her hand lies relaxed, palm-upward, on the table, index finger provocatively curled toward the officer. The hand shapes a startlingly lewd caress—though all it holds at the moment is light and air—inches from the body of the wary officer.

I can hardly believe it—but it does confirm on the simplest level what is going on between the two. Still, the painting remains unknowable, each volatile detail contradicting the next. The girl is seen in the most flattering, yet also the least flattering light possible—which is, for me, part of Vermeer's triumph.

The viewer is the complicating factor—I am the third character, addressed more and more directly as Vermeer matures. I gaze now, a little voyeuristically, over the officer's shoulder at the girl, evaluating her much as he might. Who is she? I wonder. His body language is tense, his right arm akimbo, his huge right hand massively crumpled on his right hip, where she can't see it, but I can. The officer's face is shown in three-quarter profile, from the rear—the protruding nose, the merest glint of an eye. I can't read his apparently conflicted and withheld intentions, but there's more, much more than a hint of threat in him. He makes me wonder: As a man, how often have I presented myself in such a way? How often have I been the shadow looming in a room?

And still her unguarded sweetness comes shining back. No matter how I see her, what is undeniable is the intent, native warmth of her smile, framed by the bonnet—as it is in *Woman Holding a Balance,* as it is with his other beneficent creatures. Apart from her startling flush or the apparently lewd gesture of her left hand, her face—her unguarded sweetness—is still the focal point, deepening the work by denying easy resolution. It knocks me flat.

It is a purity of love that permeates the lighted cube of space. Her right-hand edge is traced with light. Her white collar is shadowed just at the edge dun-gray, a bit darker than necessary, in order to contrast more decisively with the whitewash. Her bonnet is one of the characteristic, subliminal miracles of its type. It features a shadow on the side that is similar to the shadow-hands that gently support the heads of his later women. Folded behind the head, following the curve of the skull, it forms an illumined sliver of crescent moon. Like the more dramatic hands in the later works, this moon isn't immediately obvious, but once it is seen, it can't be unseen. In any case, this slender figment of moon seems to cup the lovely girl's skull, protecting her, cradling her with a sidelong halo.

All this, again, in service of *what*? For Vermeer doesn't follow nature, exactly, and he doesn't exactly follow light. It's the light of love he cares about: her lit face facing down the dark. Her purity, the purity of love envelops the officer too, and envelops me as well. She is not Mary Magdalene. She is no more nor less, thank God, than her mortal, bought-and-paid for self; her plaintively, lewdly beckoning hand; but she is enough. She is all there is.

The male/female relationship, Snow points out, is seldom taken as subject beyond this point. What happens now is that the solitary women take center stage, and the dialogue in the genre scenes is reconfigured between viewer and subject. The dramas embodied in the early scenes are internalized; the apparatus is stripped away. The hungering gaze of *The Girl with a Pearl Earring*, for instance, addresses me—just as I gaze back at her—with an immediacy and urgency that Vermeer had mapped out, figure by figure, in these few early works.

2. Maps

The Dutch were the world's cartographers, and maps and globes are among Vermeer's stock props. The map on the back wall in *Officer with Laughing Girl* is easily one of his best. It's an infinitely detailed depiction of seventeenth century Holland, based on a published map of the day that Vermeer probably owned (since it appears in several paintings). Looking at it, at first I don't recognize it as Holland. (Later, I will learn that the convention of orienting maps with north upward wasn't standard in Vermeer's day.) The top of the painting shows the seacoast—so that north is right, south is left. What's even more confusing to the modern eye is that the painting reverses what we think of as traditional colors for land and sea: the sea is brown, the land blue. Only the tiny sailing ships placed all over the brown Zuiderzee help identify it as water. The effect is, at least, disorienting. In *Woman in Blue Reading a Letter,* the same map is rendered completely in dark gold and sepia tones. Vermeer zooms in there, cutting off the seacoast and focusing on the aortal tributaries and marshlands toward the left of this view. In fact, the geography is still precisely rendered, although Holland becomes something entirely other: abstractly tectonic, brooding behind the hidden thoughts of the silent, reading woman, like a rippling, organic manifestation of consciousness itself.

Here, in *Officer with Laughing Girl,* the map is much clearer and more detailed, with readable inscriptions and place names. But the color reversals boggle me mentally. Everything is topsy-turvy—a secret, looking-glass world. The bottom edge of the map just grazes the top of the woman, who is positioned nearer to it in perspective. The great black hat of the officer, however, blocks a portion of it on his side. The map might be an allusion to the "real" world, open to the officer but not to the girl. That's one obvious reading. What I see, however, is the terra incognita of love.

3. Interrupted

A little farther down the South Hall is another small Vermeer, *Girl Interrupted in Her Music* (c. 1658–61). It's dim and in a very poor state of preservation. Still, I love its smoky/subaqueous vibe. It features a couple that has been studying sheet music, perhaps playing a duet. There's a still life on the table before them that includes a lute, more sheet music, a Delftware pitcher, and a glass of scarlet wine. The instruments—music itself—of course, are part of the trope. And the cavalier seems to offer an ideal, deferential sort of love—one hand on the sheet of music, almost touching the girl's right hand; the other resting lightly on the back of her chair. He's dressed in a nonthreatening gray cloak, as he stands close to her, sheltering, attentive, the opposite of the man in *Officer with Laughing Girl.* The vague background—the almost illegible painting of Cupid hanging behind the couple, on the smudged rear wall, and the chair—is badly abraded. But there are a number of very striking details: the finials on the nearer chair are especially crisp (they face inward, almost like a third presence at the table), and the pitcher is amazingly, almost photographically clear. The girl's blouse is a vivid blood red that stands out in an interior of muted blues and grays, and rhymes visually with the last of the wine in her glass.

What transforms the painting is the girl's direct glance over her left shoulder. She's a prototype for *The Girl with a Pearl Earring*, whose own gaze challenges as directly, but also ambiguously, from over her left shoulder.

But here the glance is not brimming with conflict, reproach, desire, urgency. This glance is unfazed, deadpan, straight-into-the-lens. It's not exactly a lovely face, but Vermeer insinuates loveliness in the broad-boned cheeks, the wide set of her eyes, and in her heart-shaped mouth. She looks straight at me, whoever I am, a stand-in for the painter or an intruder (or perhaps both), whom the gentleman in the painting has not yet noticed. But what is most disconcerting about her gaze is what is not expressed. There is no trace of alarm. Does she know the intruder—does she know me? Or is my presence simply nonthreatening to her? Yet there is also no sense of welcoming, no flicker of gladness or even empathy in her features. She simply stares at me, patiently, impassively.

Her eyes are dark enough to stand out of the shadows, as they mark my entrance into the scene, a scene that is about to change, I know, yet cannot know how. And it is only in the mysterious way things do stand out of the watery air—in the exquisite clarity of the still life, the hue of her blouse, the darkness of her irises—that I dimly sense what is at stake. The painting is a love song, sung in a minor key. The lesson goes on, the girl's future is unfolding, but for now—as she turns to face the painter, her familiar—she meets fate with open eyes. The sunlight fades, the phosphorescent objects gleam, and this work, like *Officer with Laughing Girl*, is not easy for me to walk away from.

The last Vermeer in the Frick, in the grand West Gallery, is a large one. *Mistress and Maid* (1666–67) is an epistolary scene, like *A Lady*

Writing, and once again features the yellow jacket with ermine trim. It depicts an elegant lady, poised with face turned in three-quarter profile away from me, with quill in hand, just as she is interrupted by the arrival of a portentous letter, delivered by a trusted and ruddy maid. It's clear it is an important letter because of how the lady's left fingertips rise involuntarily to the tip of her chin, the delicate lowering of her jaw. I love the tender expression of the maid, as if unaware of status—as if there's a sisterly bond that easily and naturally transcends every boundary between them.

I can't completely embrace this painting, and it might have to do with the fact that the background, for once, is left dark and undefined, so the figures hover in nebulous space. Some critics have assumed that the painting was unfinished simply because of this uncharacteristic background, and some, including Gowing, have even doubted the painting's attribution. Looking at it, I realize how crucial geometry is in Vermeer. The placement of figures in such exquisitely calibrated relation to each other, and to the rake of light across the textured, whitewashed wall—this is the ground that sustains the vision. Its absence here is jarring—at least it is for me, accustomed as I am by now to Vermeer's typical whitewashed wall.

But the ermine trim is astonishingly plush and convincing, as are the dramatically shadowed folds of the yellow fabric, her beaded chignon, and the exquisite translucence of her pearls. I'm amused by how the lady's handwriting on the page breaks with perspective—it doesn't slant as it should with the letter laid flat on the desk before her. Instead, the lines run vertically toward us, in order to keep the lines from blurring together. We're not meant to be conscious of this, of course, and probably most viewers aren't. It's another example of what Kees termed "photoshopping."

The West Gallery, with its two Rembrandts (*The Polish Rider* and a late self-portrait), a Velasquez, an El Greco, and a Goya, is probably as fine a roomful of Old Masters as one could find this side of the Louvre. *Mistress and Maid* hangs comfortably and nobly among such company. It's the last painting Henry Clay Frick purchased before he died.

I sit on one of two creaky, pale-green, period divans that face each other across the midst of the gallery. Above them an enormous pair of luminous Turners—the sunrise Dieppe harbor, the sunset Cologne harbor—attempt to out-dazzle each other. I rest my legs for a delicious minute, then rise and proceed through the central courtyard back to the main entrance. The restroom is down two flights of stairs, a nice, old-fashioned, white marble room. While washing my hands, I glance at the blear-eyed, scruffy, asymmetrical face in the mirror. It looks like I slept in the bus station. (Actually, it was the Leo House, a Catholic hotel in Chelsea.) But those blue eyes are steady and startlingly ferocious. My fingertips press down firmly on the edge of the sink.

I check in again with *Officer and Laughing Girl* before I leave.

4. Fifth Avenue

I cross Fifth Avenue in order to be next to the park as I float the next few blocks to the Metropolitan Museum of Art. On such a high-spirited day—the cherry trees in blossom; Stuart Little's pond a thicket of outsized, remote-controlled yachts; all the playgrounds going full-tilt—it might seem unlikely that I could simply walk next to the park and not go inside it, but I do. The rest of New York's Vermeers, the rest of America's Vermeers, are a couple of minutes away. The Met has more of them than any other museum in the world, five in all—and since the Frick and the Met are so close to each other, I can't imagine any Vermeer lover not wanting to see all in one fell swoop, as I'm in the act of doing, this sunny, kite-flying afternoon.

My left elbow occasionally grazes the stone-and-mortar park wall. The top of it is peaked like the ridge of a house, and when I touch it, it feels like sandstone—faint grit lingering on the fingertip. Swept along on a tide of gratefulness that I can't get to the bottom of, I amble purposefully. For once in my life, I'm precisely where I need to be, and I know it.

This is a little like walking through the streets of The Hague toward the Mauritshuis—toward *The Girl with a Pearl Earring*—except far better. It is as if, halfway through my journey, I find myself suspended midway on a bridge between two great collections of Vermeer, between two great museums, two worlds. I know every footstep on the root-buckled paving stones for the grace it truly is. I can go as fast or as slow as I want on this bridge of the present, so I choose to walk rather slowly.

Over the wall, in a playground there, two little girls about Sophia's age are spinning together on a tire swing—the type held by three chains, with a swivel above. They whoop and shriek, pink sweaters and pigtails whirling straight outward with centrifugal force. Suddenly, I ardently wish Sophia were here.

I do what parents do at such times: I fantasize about a trip I intend to take with her, maybe in a year or two. A classic trip to the city; why hadn't I thought of that before? But where will we go? The obvious places for kids are usually best: the Central Park Zoo, the Statue of Liberty, American Girl Place New York, a walk on the High Line. That should do it.

And yet my mind is restless. I'm still thinking about the Frick, especially about *Officer and Laughing Girl*. I'm trying to process what I've seen. I remember a phrase that Gowing uses in discussing this painting: he says it reflects an "unhappy jocularity." Perhaps he is speaking more about genre—the procuresses, the leering, drunken soldiers of the "merry company" scenes—than the actual canvas. Certainly the officer is a hugely discomfiting figure, his great bulk exaggerated by the big black hat, and his enormous, crumpled right hand. And his darkness is accentuated by placing him in such a luminous room, in front of such a luminous face.

But I wonder if I am projecting. The wine, the questionable encounter, and the girl's apparent naivety—the openness of her fetching smile, the translucent, glowing blush of her cheeks–all trouble me. The girl could hardly seem more vulnerable. There was a time I might not have felt this way. But I am older now, I've taught too many young women in my classes, and my heart's been permanently melted by Sophia's arrival in my life.

I'm floating uptown—shimmering water on my left and the copper-green roof of the boathouse—but she prevails; the face of human good prevails. I felt this at first glance, and still feel it now. I can't forget her touching gaze, the way Vermeer portrays her lazy right eye, drifting slightly out. It's the sort of observation that lingers in the mind and adds warmth to so many of his women; it makes me cherish them. I might even call the effect spiritual: she seems unfocussed in a prophetic way, seeing past what brings the officer to her, and past, perhaps, what he is capable of seeing in himself. She finds his presence riveting, it's clear, but at the same time sees straight through him, and me, to a secret apparent only to herself. Despite the built-in conflict, every orthogonal leads back to her—that guileless smile that fills the room with light.

Over the park wall, I glimpse a side-view of the colossal bronze sculpture of Alice in Wonderland rising at the far end of the pond: Alice surrounded by the Rabbit, the Hatter, the Cheshire Cat.

There is your model for random encounters, I tell myself. *There are your transformations.*

Some of Tenniel's delectably surreal drawings come to mind, the ones I pore over so happily with Sophia in my lap: Alice swimming for her life in the Pool of Tears, Alice dolefully holding a pig dressed as a baby, the outlandish Hatter at the Tea Party.

Then the sculpture is behind me. Straight ahead, I make out the oddly warted trunks of a sycamore copse—no, it's London planes— the swollen boles of their bodies slick and black as toads. The white stone flagship of museums looms beyond.

5. A Question

Upstairs in the Metropolitan Museum of Art, the first Vermeer I come to is a very early (1656–7) genre piece called *A Maid Asleep*. This one painting keeps company in a central gallery full of Dutch Masters. The other four Vermeers hang side-by-side in the last room of the wing. Maybe the curators felt *A Maid Asleep* is of a different breed altogether. It is similar to Nicholas Maes's sublime *Girl Peeling Apples* that hangs next to it here. In fact, the vocabulary of this early painting is, as Gowing writes, "not essentially different" from that of Vermeer's contemporaries.

The painting depicts a young girl, presumably a maid, at a table strewn with wineglasses, a fruit bowl, pitcher, cutlery, and other ambiguous objects. Her head nods forward, and is propped on her right hand. If we're supposed to see the girl in *Officer and Laughing Girl* as a prostitute, then we're probably supposed to see this one as a drunk. She's robust and solid, somewhat like *The Milkmaid* in stature. She's wearing a black cap and what seems an overly fancy dress of scarlet velvet. In fact, she's adrift in a sea of scarlet: what I can see of the riveted leather seatback behind her appears to be the same shade of red as her dress; the expensive, expansive Persian throw crumpled over the table is also mostly red; and a bowl before her is filled with red apples. All this deep red around her blurs the essential boundaries between that small part of her body that we can make out, and the disheveled table before her.

The background of *A Maid Asleep* is an odd one. To the right, in the background of the scene, is a partially open door, through which we view a farther, brighter room, with a covered table and mirror on a wall above it. It's an Alice-in-Wonderland-style keyhole view that lends the painting depth and light. Above the girl, to the left, there's a small corner of a painting-within-the-painting. Because the canvas is badly abraded in places, all I can make out for certain is a foot—it turns out to be the foot of the same cupid who hangs dimly in the background of *Girl Interrupted in Her Music,* and who will finally appear clearly in *A Lady Standing at a Virginal.* Here, the obscure foot can barely be made out. Lying just to the right of it is a discarded and shadowy white mask, propped upright.

It's thrilling to me to see so many motifs make their first appearance and to recognize them as such: the cupid, the mask (which also reappears dramatically in the late *The Art of Painting),* the mirror, the finials, even what seems to be the corner of a map hanging on the wall toward the right. Here is the vocabulary—all of it, like the cupid's foot, making an agonizingly tentative and cryptic entrance into the painter's gaze.

Critics have not been kind to this woman. Arthur Wheelock characterizes her appearance as "melancholic," "despondent," even "slothful." In person, her presence is remarkably expressive, but expressive of nothing in particular, the heaviness and pallor of her face vividly registering the rush of passion, alcohol, or simply the headiness of youth. After all, she's dressed sexily in red, with décolletage, framed by the cupid behind, and by the table rather wildly set with wineglasses before her. I can see the nature of her sleep as a drunken stupor, a fantasy, a catnap, or even as a sham, a pretense at sleep as a lover approaches—perhaps this is what the mask implies. But I keep changing my mind, as I did with *Officer and Laughing Girl*, and never can decide. And in my own relationships, no matter how often I sift through my memories, it's nearly impossible to tell who was the pursuer, who was the pursued.

Radiographs show that Vermeer once included a gentleman standing in the farther room, and a dog in the lower right, staring toward the man. The dog was covered up with a leather-upholstered Spanish chair, with a rather vaguely realized pillow with gold piping propped against it. How would these figures have affected the emotional chemistry of the painting, had they remained? What happens when you strip away such props? But perhaps it isn't so easy to strip them away. In painting out the dog in the doorway, what if the painter allows the partially open door *itself* to function as a sentinel; what if he decides to let the lion-head finials of the chair present themselves as they do in later works? In painting out the man in the far room, what if he allows the mirror there to assert its depths and truth-telling function in a way that foretells the mirrors in *The Music Lesson* or *Woman Holding a Balance?* And though one must take the artist's final version of a painting as authoritative, perhaps nothing can ever be unpainted anyway, each image inextricably connected to the one before, back to the first thought or daub of paint on the canvas. Perhaps this discovery is the true thrill of the painting: Vermeer discovering how to unpaint the genre scene, uncovering, as he does, its latent resonance.

On the table, one object especially begins to bother me. It has a silver handle on each end, and lies diagonally amongst the clutter of the still-life—glass and chiffon. I can't, for the life of me, figure it out. It looks like a very short walking stick.

As I'm standing there, a young girl, a college freshman perhaps, approaches. She's wearing really, *really* tattered jeans and a black T-shirt. She's plump; her hair is cut in a severe and dramatically black-tinted pageboy. When she comes to *A Maid Asleep*, she takes a creased black Moleskine journal out of her back pocket, opens it, and begins to flick/flick rapid notes and drawings. The journal is already filled cover-to-cover, and stuffed to the gills with extra scraps of paper. I give her a moment, and then, because I decide she is clearly smart, ask: "There's one thing I can't identify. Do you have any idea what this is?" I trace the silver-handled object with the tip of my thumb. (Unfortunately, I come too close to the surface of the uncovered canvas, and a guard promptly appears. Warning nod; apologetic nod.)

She steps up and regards the object steadfastly for a minute. Bites her lip. Her eyes are quick and nearly black—like the eyes of *Girl Interrupted in Her Music*. Finally, she glances at me and shakes her head.

Thanks. See you, I say with a nod.

6. Room 12

Room 12 has an end-of-the-rainbow feeling. It's spacious, perfectly lit, with a comfortably cushioned bench, where I can sit and contemplate Vermeer's women as long as I like.

Together on one wall, right to left, are *Young Woman with a Water Pitcher, Study of a Young Woman,* and *Woman with a Lute.* These are mature works, from the 1660s. On its own, on the wall on the left, is *Allegory of Faith.* I'm moving slowly from right to left, starting with the remarkably well-preserved *Young Woman with a Water Pitcher*, the first of the thirteen Vermeers to enter the United States (in 1889).

It is a painting of great clarity and harmony, one of Gowing's "pearl pictures." A bonneted woman at her toilet stands in the streaming light, her left hand resting on a gilded pitcher, her right hand partially concealed by the exquisite, blue-tinted leaded casement she seems to be opening. Walter Liedtke, a curator of the Met, speaks for most when he calls this woman an "icon of domesticity." There is a map behind her, a jewelry box (with a strand of pearls just visible), and a carpeted table before her: it's an upper-class scene, a cousin of *Woman Holding a Balance.* The shimmering pitcher and basin have an optically determined, liquid quality, like the chandelier in *An Artist in His Studio.* They dominate the space; they glimmer, neither near nor far, like objects in a dream.

Gowing, though, makes a unique and controversial assessment that cuts to the quick: he calls this painting the "most primitive" of its type. He says that Vermeer "falters when the crucial detail" (the head) is reached. And compared to so many of Vermeer's other heads, with their powerful claims on my attention, this one does look rather lifeless to me. I realize that this is partly the point: she's an ideal, blocked out in light and shade. Still, in contrast to the magical equilibrium of *The Milkmaid* and *Woman Holding a Balance* the figure in this painting seems all too settled to me. She stands a little stiffly and doll-like, a figure of sunlight, lacking a distinct physiognomy.

That can't be said about the painting next to it. *Study of a Young Woman* is a head of comparable dimensions to *The Girl with a Pearl Earring,* and is often characterized as a likely pendant (or companion painting) for the earlier work. Many believe that the sitters for both paintings were daughters of the painter. It is also, as John Michael Montias dryly wrote, "a portrait if ever there was one." Her wide-set eyes, short nose, straight mouth, and jutting jaw are anything but idealized, or conventionally pretty. Yet the tone of the painting toward its subject is tender, even reverent. The characterization here could hardly be more different from that of *The Girl with a Pearl Earring.* Instead of the other's erotic intensity, this one is all softness and innocence, her enormous, liquid eyes brimming with dream. She is someone's sister; she is someone's daughter. I walk away unscathed from her, which might be the point. Unscathed, but not untouched.

Moving to the left, *Woman with a Lute* contains a single figure who seems to be the same girl with wide-set eyes depicted in *Study of a Young Woman,* though this painting allows her more distance and is more flattering to her. What's unusual about the painting is how far Vermeer has gone to shelter the girl: by the sentinel finials in the foreground, dramatically enlarged in perspective; by the bulk of the table she sits behind; by the heap of blue tablecloth; and by the lute itself, that she holds before her chest as she tunes it, glancing sidelong, oblivious, into the north light streaming in. Though she is alone for now, the lute, the strewn sheet music, and the viola de gamba on the floor suggest imminent passion—as in *Girl Interrupted in Her Music.* Like that painting, this one seems dim and subaqueous and is badly abraded, especially in the foreground, which is very murky. And also like that painting, this one also has a few very well preserved bright touches, especially the huge pearl earrings worn by the girl, her pearl necklace, and the yellow, ermine-trimmed jacket, making yet another appearance. There's an extraordinary wistfulness in these details. Her dreamy, expectant mood as she watches for her suitor, her relaxed, unselfconscious pose and the grace of her fingers turning the keys of the lute, all capture the anticipatory joy of romance better than anything else I've seen.

But this also has to be the most damaged Vermeer I've seen, and it's probably the most damaged Vermeer in the world. Gowing pronounces the painting a "ruin." And of course, he is right, it is a shame. But then again, I remember Gowing's insights on *The Girl with a Pearl Earring.* Toward the back of his book, he discusses the way this image, this beauty, is constructed, even reprinting a radiograph that shows the underlying form of white lead, a blunt, mysterious shape quite different from the finished head. This is, for me, the most thrilling moment in his book, leading to such rapturous passages as: "the radiography of painting has never shown a form in itself as wonderful as this." What the radiograph reveals is the bare notation of her glance, her being—the candescent gleam of her eye, the architecture of bone, the mouth in all its nakedness, its need—laid down as it is seen, not yet translated into something we call a "girl." Here, it is clear, if Vermeer ever used the camera, he used it. There is no drawing, no design, only light transcribed on the visible weave of the canvas. Much of what the painting tells us is a result of the thin, opaque layers that bring her conventional prettiness into being; much of what we feel, however, comes from this naked image, the primal record just concealed beneath.

It might seem perverse when I suggest that paintings like *Woman with Lute* or *Girl Interrupted in Her Music* or *The Girl with a Pearl Earring* benefit somehow, for me, from their poor state of conservation. I don't feel exactly that way: of course it is tragic that some of the Vermeer masterpieces are so badly damaged. Paintings aren't like the Grand Canyon, which owes its sublimity to erosion. And yet a Vermeer is a Vermeer all the way down, like the face beneath the face in the head of *The Girl with a Pearl Earring:* each brushstroke yoked to the one before and after. So what can be truly lost? Perhaps it's enough to say that the damages to the painting are unfortunate—as are the damages any of us receives in the travels of our lives. And yet such damages can also be a testament to the power of the original vision, the deepest source of beauty.

In any case, my favorite painting here, in Room 12, has somehow shed about ninety per cent of its paint. The contours of the woman's head—across the top of her forehead and hairdo—appear to have been deliberately smudged, not by the process of time so much as by two powerful thumbs pushing in hard, as if to drive her outline into the whiteness of the wall behind. The lute itself, especially, has been ravaged—reduced to the rough shape of body and neck in the woman's hands. I make out one or two of its keys—she is tuning the instrument, string by string—but not the strings themselves, and the sound hole is more a mere gesture or shadow than image. (Later this year, I'll see *The Guitar Player*, in London's Kenwood House. It's an extraordinary example of what Vermeer can do with musical instruments—among its six strings of varying thicknesses, one can even make out which seem to be quivering as they are strummed, and which are not!)

But if this lute and the woman herself are mere ghosts, they are resonant ghosts. It's true she is barely here, the body of the lute, and all it might signify, held lightly, lightly, in her wraithlike hands. As she keeps one ear on the note she plucks—as she carefully tunes the pitch of the string—she looks sidelong out through the window, into the watery radiance. One might think it's an expectant look, and the woman's dress and her pearls seem to support this—but it also seems a natural reflex of consciousness, a flicker of feeling that leads her sidelong into the distance. Her dreamy, wide-set eyes and smudged head underscore her vulnerability, the quick of a moment lit upon blue shadows.

And that leaves *Allegory of Faith*, hanging, logically, on a separate wall to the left. It's a splendid if overwrought work that showcases Vermeer's touch with the transparency of the pendant glass globe, his characteristic highlights on the golden chalice, and one of his most baroque black-and-white checked marble floors. Dazzling, really. Not to mention the sumptuously rich tapestry in the foreground, very similar to the trappings of *The Art of Painting*, which is probably the prototype for this later work. Faith, the central figure, is lifted from Ripa's Iconology, in which she is described as "a seated lady . . . her feet resting on Earth."

This seated lady swoons operatically. It's unsettling to see Vermeer's staggering technique, the fearsome clarity of his imagination enlisted in service of . . . what? Some speculate that the painting was commissioned by a Catholic patron—probably one who had seen *The Art of Painting* and asked for a religious version of it, a translation of sorts. Late in his life, with his huge family and the collapsing art market, Vermeer might have felt obligated to try such a thing. If it is a cold, impersonal sort of vision, then that is in keeping with the tradition of the Leiden *finschilders*, or painters of small, detailed works. It seems hardly a Vermeer at all—unlike *Mistress and Maid*, for instance, which seems so clearly a Vermeer to me, so subtle and domestic, despite its unfinished state.

On my way out, just as I'm re-entering and crossing the large room containing *A Woman Sleeping*, a tour group enters from the opposite side, led by a somewhat rumpled, pleasantly professorial guide. He assembles the group before the Vermeer, and begins talking about Dutch genre scenes. I hang around at the back of the circle, biding my time happily for a couple of minutes, until he asks for questions. I step out, trace the mysterious object in the still life with a fingertip (a few feet in front of the canvas, this time), and ask, "Can you please tell me what this is?"

He has thought about this before and, both nodding and smoothing the corners of his gray mustache, defines it authoritatively: "It's a pair of knives, lying tip to tip." He enthusiastically parses it with his thumb. He wants me, a fellow Vermeer lover, to understand. The others in the group are invisible for this moment. "See?" he says. I feel an immediate click of satisfaction and thank him. How typical for Vermeer to give us only what the eye takes in, I think, not what we comprehend—our comprehension is not Vermeer's concern. It's as if his goal is to picture life as God himself might see it, without human interference. And as if he knows this is what we really want. I glance again at the painting—the open door and all it beckons toward, the pristine emptiness of the room beyond—and turn to leave.

7. The Green Dragon Club

I retrace my steps in early evening, this time inside the wall. I've decided to meander through the park, to take a better look at Alice in Wonderland and the Stuart Little pond, and then I'll go on past the Children's Zoo toward the Leo House in Chelsea. It's cooler now, the light is flatly filtering through the groves, and most of the children are gone. I've got my camera out—not for myself, but for the photos I'll show to Sophia. When I can say, *I'd like to take you here someday.*

As I walk, though, I'm remembering an old, brown, bison-shaped leather armchair, an icon of my own childhood. After dinner, we three small boys would wrestle for our favorite perch on the arms— we'd ride them, buckaroo style—and both baby girls would plop down in Dad's lap. We called it The Green Dragon Club—those mirror-bright nights, collapsible characters of a collapsible world— my happiest memory of my father. (After he died, at the family memorial in his Unitarian church in Columbia, I suddenly recalled The Green Dragon Club, and described it at the gathering.)

Maybe it didn't seem so great at the time, back then, all that squirming and shoving for position, but the instant Dad adjusted his bifocals and began to read, that house was transformed. There, in the center of the room, a big rabbit hopped past Alice, dreaming as she lay by the riverbank. And then, as we watched, "the Rabbit actually took a watch out of its waistcoat-pocket," and my father laughed his sonorous (and often phlegmatic) belly laugh, and each of us in that big chair soared.

Arriving at the base of the huge, ensemble sculpture, I circle it as I take shots of Sophia's favorite characters at leisure. A close-up of the Dormouse, a close-up of Alice.

Poor Alice, never the right size Alice! A confounding bottle commands her: DRINK ME. A confounding cake commands her: EAT ME. But nothing ever works as it should; she never quite fits the Looking-Glass World. Children grasp Alice's dilemma intuitively since they, too, find themselves in unstable bodies. They, too, never quite fit.

Back home, I have an ugly, but supremely comfortable beige Lazy-Boy recliner. (It was one of the items Sara didn't want when she left.) In the reading hour after dinner and after bath time, Sophia and I take to this chair just as I once took to my own father's overstuffed leather armchair. We've started calling this hour The Green Dragon Club—that was Sophia's idea, in fact. She wedges her tiny, pajama-clad hips blissfully on the left side next to mine, and I encircle her with my left arm, holding the evening's book in both hands—the left half of it on her right thigh, the right half of it on my left. As I begin to read, she traces the words with her right index finger, as if she could control the pace of the story thus (and she can). Shadowy figures materialize before us—the March Hare and the Cheshire Cat float a few feet beyond our toes.

HOW IT WORKS

There's only England left on my itinerary. Only four more Vermeers.

I often think back on that afternoon I sat outside of the Rijskmuseum and hatched the outline of these travels. And yet, despite the research and planning and trips and the poems I've written, I've never felt like the author of any of it. I'm more like a character who walks from chapter to chapter. Each painting waits like a room furnished for me and me alone, a spell conjured for me and me alone, an instrument strummed so softly that only I can hear it.

From the outside, it might appear mundane, if not dull: teaching at a small, Southern university; single and sober, etcetera. But with all of the planning leading up to each ecstatic trip, this semi-secret life occupies nearly all of my interest and, if not for my weekends with Sophia, nearly all of my love. Meanwhile, I'm also doing what I've done since 1983: I go to A. A. Without which I'd be defenseless against the death of my first wife or the divorce of my second, or practically any major difficulty. Without which I wouldn't be looking at art at all, because I'd be dead.

I attended my first few meetings in rehab, in the dilapidated Mid-Missouri Mental Health Center, which no longer exists. Like virtually everyone else, I wasn't there by choice. I was stubborn and indignant. I didn't think I belonged there—either in rehab, or in A. A. But over the following days, I paid attention to the others in the meetings, to the ones with some sobriety. I stared at them, transfixed, as if they were zoo animals. They were smiling and relaxed and clear-eyed—everything I was not. So it didn't take long for me to realize that I had nothing to lose. I decided to follow their suggestions.

I had one relapse—a two-day bender—six months after treatment. (My sobriety date is December 30, 1983.) One evening, as I walked home from my dishwashing job, I passed a popular college bar, a place I used to like. I could hear the laughter welling irresistibly from within. I stopped for a moment, thought of my life, my job, my tiny, rented room, and did not go in. I was twenty-eight years old. I walked past that bar the next day, too. But on the third day I went inside.

I inhaled the first beer without tasting it. But I couldn't stop. I went home, got every dollar I'd saved, and it was on. This was during a blizzard, the city encased in ice. Early Friday morning, after the bars closed, I fell hard in the middle of a street on the edge of campus, and couldn't get up. Three times I tried and slipped and fell. Then I thought, why bother? I felt comfortable lying there.

But after a few minutes, I did get up. I scrabbled to all fours and lurched off toward my room. Beginning the next day, I got a new home group, picked up a new white chip (claiming my second one-day chip was one of the hardest things I've done). After that meeting, I found a new sponsor, a man about the age I am today, a charismatic attorney with ten years of sobriety. Bill Wilson, one of our co-founders, wrote: "Because of our kinship in suffering, our channels of contact have always been charged with the language of the heart." That's what I felt then; that's still the draw for me now. Newcomers tend to think that it's the lucky or the smart ones who survive. But survival has little to do with wisdom or experience. It's the beaten ones who make it, the ones who can truly give up honestly.

All through this year of my divorce, I double up on my meetings. One a day, and sometimes more. I volunteer at the nearby medium-security men's prison, where the simple fact that I leave, when the meeting ends, lends me a special status. In my home group here in Wilmington, I try to be one of the ones who's always present, one of the "old-timers." Sometimes I don't say anything, but simply show up early, help make coffee, set up the folding chairs and banners and whatnot—there are many small, comforting things to do.

Meetings are pretty much the same wherever you go. We draw our coffee from the big cylindrical coffeemakers in churches, treatment centers, or prisons; we listen to the Preamble. Then, for an hour, we listen, half appalled and/or half in stitches to stories of people finding their way out of colossal setbacks, devastated lives. "What we were like, what happened, what we are like now." At the end of most meetings, somebody reads the Ninth Step Promises ("Are these extravagant promises? We think not!"). Someone hands out chips, beginning with white. Then we circle up, hold hands, and say the Lord's Prayer, or the Third Step Prayer, or "a prayer of your choice in silence." Afterwards, some of us shake hands and talk, while others put away chairs and books, or mop the floors. We old-timers seek out newcomers—especially those still in rehab or halfway houses—and offer encouragement along with our phone numbers. During the winter of my divorce, two newcomers ask me to sponsor them. Eventually, after long discussions, I tell each of these young men it would be an honor, just as my first sponsor once told me.

However it works, A. A. works. I could relapse again tomorrow. It happens. But I stay involved, and I've never been more thankful for A. A. than I am today. No matter how lousy I might feel when I walk into a meeting, I feel lighter when I leave. For twenty-five years now, this is my secret weapon. This is the story beneath the story.

LONDON

[*May*]

1. Descent

Once again, a turbulent crossing; once again, no sleep. We descend at dawn over an island sealed beneath low clouds. Here and there, clearings loom—emerald patches of heath and hedgerows, villages clustered around their steeples—ragged breaks in a sleepy stream of thought.

It's mid-May, a little over a year since my first trip to Amsterdam. My spring semester is done, and with Sophia still in school for two more weeks, I have an open window for my final trip. I'm filing off the plane with Gowing and Snow, umbrella and notebook packed in my shoulder bag, nothing that I won't need.

I take the express from Gatwick to Victoria, and emerge from the tube an hour later at Russell Square. I reconnoiter, cross the street into the park, and order a café au lait in the Russell Square Park Café. It's London, chilly and damp. I gaze warily across the deserted park. As much as I've contemplated this trip, I haven't been able to settle on a plan. I've got just four days in which to see four Vermeers, and I want to get it right.

The two late masterpieces in the National Gallery are *A Lady Standing at a Virginal* and *A Lady Seated at a Virginal*. They are virtual twins—critics like Snow have labeled them "explicit pendants." From the beginning of my journey, this pair seemed the natural endpoint, because they are the endpoint of Vermeer's line of solitary women.

The other two Vermeers in England are *The Music Lesson,* in the Royal Collection, and *Lady with a Guitar,* in the Kenwood House in Hampstead. The first of these is a bit of an anomaly among England's Vermeers, not only because it's an earlier work (from around the time of *Woman Holding a Balance*), but also because it is a group scene, a conversation piece that connects the casual and traditional subject matter of *Officer and Laughing Girl* to the intensely private manner of *An Artist in His Studio. The Music Lesson* depicts an enigmatic romantic couple. The girl playing the virginal, her sinuous back facing toward us, the man standing in rapt attention beside her—and the intense dynamic, the magic—are comparable in the oeuvre only to *An Artist in His Studio.*

I let the counterman pick the change from my hand. I don't know where he's from, but he's wearing a purple silk turban, and has alarmingly lush eyebrows. I ask him how to find Cartwright Gardens, where my hotel is located. From behind the counter, he unfolds a map and traces out each turn, each blind alley, with his large thumb, because it's very close, but "it's complicated," he says. That's how I find myself bumping along through leafy Bloomsbury, suitcase in tow, trying to follow the counterman's directions, while simultaneously planning my stay.

Chronologically, I probably ought to start with *The Music Lesson,* in Her Majesty's Royal Collection, at Windsor Castle. It's one of the most beautiful and distant and poetic of all the works. It's the one I'm most longing to see. Then maybe I should simply skip the woman at Kenwood, since in photos it seems greenish, off-center, and hard to relate to the other Vermeers. I plan to focus on the National Gallery ladies, the proper conclusion to my project.

My room at the Jenkins Hotel isn't ready. I stash my luggage between two set tables in the breakfast room downstairs and go for an aimless stroll. The garish smear of Leicester Square marquees in afternoon rain; graven names of poets in the Abbey; grace of anonymity. Standing on Westminster Bridge, I silently recall one of my favorite sonnets: "Earth has not anything to show more fair ..." Wordsworth's note to the poem states it was "Written on the roof of a coach, on my way to France." Meanwhile, for me, the decorous, wrought-iron darkness is deepening along the Thames. I arrive at the North Sea Fish Market a few minutes before it closes, just in time to order take-out—a huge, fresh slab of cod sprawled over a mawful of chips, with a splash of malt vinegar. I wolf down the steaming, flaky cod as I wander Gray's Inn Road past King's Cross, then back to Cartwright Gardens. I retrieve my suitcase, climb the stairs to my tiny room, and drop at once into dreamless sleep.

2. Windsor Castle

My breakfast is "full English" (eggs, mushrooms, bangers, beans). I decide, over my eggs, that I can't think about the other three paintings until I've seen *The Music Lesson*. A refill of coffee, and I'm eagerly off. Within fifteen minutes, changing from tube to train at Waterloo Station, I'm rolling out of London, out of the mouth of a long, dark tunnel and into the blinding sun, toward Windsor, toward the magical painting. I admire the gabled roofs, the cock-eyed chimneys, and the narrow little gardens behind the suburban row houses west of town. Then I burrow into Gowing again: "In *The Music Lesson*, instead of human matter, the chief object of the painter's scrutiny is the great perspective."

It's true that the figures appear far at the back of an unusually deep version of Vermeer's room. Zoomed-in on my laptop, they look small and remote, and the face of the man appears unreachably lost, on the other side of rapture.

In a half hour I make out the castle from far across the Thames Valley, the great Round Tower dominating the river bluffs and the town of Eton. The Union Jack flies above, which means the queen isn't here. I file off the train, and within a few hundred feet stop for coffee—there is a tasteful, high-end, indoor/outdoor row of tourist shops tucked in beneath the gates. I sip a frothy latte. Then I make the short climb to Windsor.

The entrance ramps guide me into a ticket office/information center/security check building. While buying my ticket, I ask the civil servant, in his bright blue uniform, where I can find Vermeer's *The Music Lesson*. He says there are no Vermeers at Windsor. I feel a stab of catch-22 panic; I hope he's wrong. It's a big castle, I think. While running my card, he tries his best to explain the nature of the Royal

Collection—in which relatively few paintings, at any given time, are shown to the public, and those that are shown rotate among the royal galleries at the whim of the queen. After I'm seated inside, next to the information desk, he disappears downstairs to make some calls, to find out about the painting. It's his lunch break anyway, he says. He'll be right back.

The second he's gone, a small voice from somewhere speaks clearly. "We have the same tastes, you and I." A tiny, pixie-ish docent sitting behind the counter, swivels toward me. She's less than five feet tall, with short, silvery hair and angelic, watery blue eyes. I hadn't even noticed her before.

"I fell in love with Vermeer when I was eighteen, in Amsterdam," she almost whispers, fixing me with an intense gaze. "The instant I saw *The Milkmaid*."

"Same here," I say. "In the Rijksmuseum."

She says she had heard on the radio that very morning that *The Music Lesson* is in fact coming to Windsor in a few days; she's excited because she'd always wanted to see it. "I can't wait," she confides.

After a few minutes, the guard returns to report that no one has answered his calls.

"But you might as well see the castle as long as you're here," she says. "It's magnificent."

Visiting the "proud keep of Windsor" entails a constant climb— it was built that way to make it easier to defend. You enter through St. George's Gate, and then loop clockwise uphill around the base of the Round Tower toward the State Apartments, where most of the treasures are to be seen. The motte is fifty feet tall, now a steeply terraced slope, with scenic little falls sidestepping brink to brink through ornamental oaks. The old tower on top carries the weight of Arthurian legend (some consider Windsor Hill the site of the original Round Table), and was built by Edward III for the Knights of the Royal Garter. Halfway around, I stop, glancing back into the Lower Ward, at St. George's Chapel, with its Gothic spires and vaults— which Ruskin calls "a very visible piece of romance"—along with the Curfew Tower, the cloisters, and the park-like common.

But I take all of this in rather sullenly. My thoughts are elsewhere. What to do about *The Music Lesson*? I have only two and a half days left; I don't want to miss it.

In the State Apartments, I pass through the room housing Queen Mary's Dollhouse, an immense scale model with working lifts, plumbing, and electricity. Soon I'll wander the Drawings Gallery, with its several pieces by Leonardo Da Vinci, through stateroom after stateroom, wing after wing on a scale I have never seen before—an impenetrable hive of empire. Yet, while still in the Dollhouse room, I happen to overhear, coming through the handset of a lady guard, a voice asking to talk to "the gentleman interested in Vermeer." I step forward, and she hands me the big, walkie-talkie style phone. It is the first guard, reporting that *The Music Lesson* would be on display at Windsor beginning next week.

"I'll be gone," I say. Now I know, the other three paintings will have to suffice.

"Well, at least we got cracking," he says.

I pass through quickly, in a blur, the hundred staterooms, reception halls for centuries of monarchs, diplomats, presidents; the drawing rooms, armories, bedchambers, and so on; out and out through the Norman Gate again, down to the Lower Ward. In St. George's Chapel, I admire the choir, where the Order of the Garter convenes, then pause for another moment, impressed by the stiff upright pews, the magnificently carved woodwork above.

In the Chapel's excellent gift shop, I pick out several gifts for Sophia—a long blue peacock quill pen, a dragon pendant, a hammered pewter spoon—and then I'm out through the Henry XVIII Gate into the street.

It's already two o'clock and I'm famished, so I look for something promising among the cafés on High Street. A conical candle in a boutique shopfront catches my eye. It's like the one I'd bought for Sophia in Delft, except sparkly and white, and I have to have it. A block or two later, a sidewalk blackboard in front of a butcher/rotisserie advertises "minted lamb" in a sideways scrawl, and that sounds almost too perfect. Inside, the counterman says, "Sorry, mate. All outa lamb! 'Ow bout a spit-roasted gammon knuckle? It'll fill you up!"

"Okay," I say. "One, uh, gammon knuckle, and a Diet Coke—I mean, Coke Light."

I sit on a nearby bench in the street outside, and open the paper bag. It's pig, as it turns out—an outsized, meaty hock the likes of which I hope never to see again. The skin crisped brown and granular with salt, the first bite a shock of spurting grease. Tender fists of smoky, fat meat tear from the bone with each ravenous bite. It's horribly, unspeakably good. Beneath a white, stone-haunted sky, what else can I do? I tuck into the roast hog, washing it down with deep swigs of soda, and when I'm completely, almost sickeningly satiated, I stuff the bone and the can back into the bag, and return to my hotel.

3. Kenwood House

On Saturday morning, I ride the lift to ground level at Hampstead Station, step out into a vicious wind, then turn to the right straight into it, straight up steep Heath Street. Almost immediately the rain slices through my sweater, and my black umbrella detonates, so I begin to look for shelter. Half a block uphill, in front of Heath Street Baptist Church, an elderly lady in a bright aqua cardigan is fumbling with a blackboard in the doorway: Saturday Morning Coffee/11 am–1pm/Coffee & Biscuits 40p. I duck in right behind her, just as she turns back into the warmth inside the vestibule.

It's a pleasantly musty nineteenth-century sanctuary, not large. "Care to join us for coffee?" the lady asks, smoothing her platinum hair.

"Yes, please," I say, and take a seat at one of the three card tables set with tablecloths and silk flowers.

"How do you take it?" she asks.

"Cream and sugar, please."

"One lump or two?"

"Two."

Hoping the storm will blow over soon, I stir my coffee, bite into a buttery shortbread cookie, and ask her about the church's most impressive feature, its stained glass. "Original," she remarks. She speaks quietly of the congregation's Sunday dinners for the homeless. I can see what the church means to her—everything. I pass an inexplicably joyful half-hour here, and then the rain has stopped. I'm off across the misting heath, until I come to the sign for the Kenwood House.

The approach to the estate is a winding lane through dripping, rain-drenched woods. I go through what appears to be the back door, get directions to *The Guitar Player,* and walk through room after room of not-quite dilapidated Victorian splendor. Finally, just past the roped-off library (which has often been a Merchant/Ivory film set), I come to Lord Iveagh's dining room. The floorboards are quite worn, a bit squeaky, with a worn Ushak carpet. Everything in the room dates from 1800–1820, the majestic Regency chandelier hanging beneath a ceiling high as a school cafeteria. Scarlet patterned velvet walls, carved gilt curtain rods the size of railroad ties. The centerpiece of the room is the iconic Rembrandt self-portrait of 1661; in fact, the curtains and walls have been color-matched to the blood-red tunic Rembrandt is wearing. I read the placard that tells how Rembrandt revised the self-portrait (painted in a mirror, as usual) by touching up his elderly, poverty-stricken, disheveled image later. He also "corrected" the reflected image optically—switching the hand holding the paintbrush from left to right, for instance.

Then I turn toward my right, toward the sunny windows and the wall containing the Vermeer. There are twenty paintings in the room, whose gilt frames coordinate with the other furnishings. The glaring exception is *The Guitar Player,* with its matte-black frame. But even from across the room, the gilt frame of the painting-within-in-the-painting stands out clearly. It's another of the artist's stylized yet convincing gilt frames—hashed together of gold pointillés—that conveys a strong, intuitive impression of the minute details it actually lacks.

The woman in *The Guitar Player* reminds me of the lute-player in the Met. Both girls look to their right, out of the painting, as they sit and strum; the implication in both cases is that they play for an absent but possibly nearby lover. The lute-player gazes dreamily into the light, her face illumined though the paint is worn; this girl glances away from the light, her face darkened yet livid. The girl in New York concentrates as she tunes the lute—she seems to gaze idly out the window, or else she gazes toward God and plays for Him. The guitar-player looks toward another, who is in the room listening with her, and she plays for him. Both girls wear pearl earrings and the same fur-trimmed, yellow jacket. Both sit toward the left of the painting, but the guitar-player carries imbalance and asymmetry to an extreme, and seems to move, to lean and turn as I look, almost as if Vermeer were consciously rebelling against the stillness and serenity of his own work. It is a shock, and yet I recognize the gnawing desire to do something, anything, differently from what one has done before—to *be* someone other than what one has paid the price to become.

Her cheeks are flushed a gaudy, pinkish-orange. The hue seems pointedly artificial compared to the blush of the earlier girls. Her dark, Picasso-like eyes are almond-shaped. The slightly protuberant peak of the forehead is outlined with a very bright highlight, like the uppermost angle of her left cheek and the side of her nose. The face, finally, seems almost brutally rendered. The blurred curls of her fancy, up-to-the-minute hairdo are rendered in fluid, corkscrew brushstrokes. The cut-off right elbow seems the gesture of another artist altogether, if not another century.

Yet there are passages of exquisitely precise description: the illusionism of the glowing pearls, the velvety decadence of the spotted ruff. And the guitar, of course, receives the full treatment—its crisp, staccato, black-and-white inlay that edges both the body and fingerboard lends hard definition to the overall vision. The heart of the painting, the luscious trompe-l'oeil sound hole, is positioned directly over the center of the woman's body. Her hands carry the burden of expression for her. The curves and segments of her left fingers are composed of unmediated daubs or lozenges of reflected light—an effect that makes the fingers seem even more ethereal than they might in a more literal approach. I marvel at her left hand unconsciously caressing the neck, as each fingertip presses down into each note. The right hand, her most "realistic" feature, is caught as the sound unfolds, the shadow of her extended little finger cast on the guitar the instant she plucks it. But the sound is not simply expressed through a careful blurring of the middle strings. It vibrates everywhere: through the luminous softness of her hands and forearms in motion, the slight clench of her jaw as she concentrates, the lyrical afterthought of her curls. It radiates out through all the colors, tone on tone, through the silver-on-silver folds of her satin dress as it drapes and clings to her right knee. Out through the folds of the yellow jacket, dark gold on a ground of luminous gold, through the gilt frame's pointillés of luminous gold on a ground of darker gold.

And again, there's a darkened window, but on the right this time. The angle of light, from over the painter's right shoulder is direct, uncomfortably direct, and in the context of the oeuvre seems almost willfully perverse. The way in which we're encouraged to stare straight into her face seems to veer as far as possible away from the discretion Vermeer has habitually shown to his women. Perhaps also because of the direct, single-sourced light, there's a modern and garish intensity to the style—the greenish tinge of her upper chest, the mask-like face all shadow and glare and blush.

Not another soul is here. Rembrandt, Vermeer, and myself.

But, no matter how long I look, for me, *The Guitar Player* remains a disconcerting painting. Energy is concentrated in the left half of the painting, radiating toward the right, but the woman glances the other way. She's right here, knees at my fingertips, with nothing in between, and yet she has nothing to do with me. Nor does she play for herself—this creature of darkness—but for another, whom I cannot see.

4. The Man in the Oilskin Parka

I'm sitting on the settee in the middle of the room when an American, probably in his thirties, strides in. He casually makes a beeline toward the Vermeer in front of me. He's wearing a dark-green British oilskin parka, with a matching wide-brim rain hat. He's slender, with good looks to match his crisp, appropriate clothes. I nod in a dreamy muse. He leans solicitously for a while, checking back with me a couple of times to make sure he's not interfering with my view. He's a bit self-conscious; he makes too much of it. When he apologizes for disturbing me, I say, "No, it's all right. Go ahead; I'll be here for a while." I gaze at his back.

After a few minutes of close study, he comes back to the center of the room and stands beside me. "Beautiful, isn't it," he says. "I've never seen another like it."

"Yeah," I say. "But it's not a Vermeer."

"Oh, yes," he says. "It *is*. It *is* a Vermeer." He looks at me with faint alarm.

After a nervous moment, I try again. "That's not what I meant. I mean it's just so *odd*. Why he placed her so far off-center . . . and with that greenish pallor, she's so unappealing."

But I have spoken too quietly (as I often do), and he says, "Yes, the color makes her so appealing. There's usually something in the foreground, too, something in front of them, as if to protect them," he adds. "But not this time."

"The lion-head chair-backs," I say. As I say it, I realize there's a single lion-head behind the guitar player, reduced to a simple, dark silhouette. Still, to me, the repertoire—the windows, the chair-backs, and Vermeer's whole dynamic language—seems shuttered in these last great works.

"Or the table with the Persian carpet in *The Music Lesson*," he says, "which really adds depth when you see it in person."

"You've seen *that*?" I ask, suddenly alert again. "I walked all over Windsor Castle looking for that painting two days ago."

"I saw it last week, at Buckingham Palace. In the Queen's Gallery," he says with a shrug. He pauses and looks at me. "Around the left side of the palace."

I thank him, smiling: he cannot know how much he has helped me.

After he leaves, I give it another half hour.

When these travels began, I was pretty sure which Vermeers appealed to me most strongly. The work that reached out to me was the same early to mid-career work that reaches so many others—the lovely, pensive women and the two landscapes. I came to London curious about how I'd react to the later works and to what seems to be a falling off.

The feeling I struggle with is not disappointment in *The Guitar Player,* but a vertigo-like sense of disorientation. It isn't simply that the light we didn't even know we were looking for (and yet so powerfully find in Vermeer) isn't there anymore. In the later work, the faces are not simply unlit, they are dark. Even the windows that would have lit the faces are shuttered. The terms of the experiment have changed; the language has changed. Even the famous stillness has changed, so that what is captured is not a face at all, but the blur of a sidelong glance, reverberating through space.

Musical instruments have moved to the fore. Here, the numinous guitar dominates the composition. Virginals and the viola da gamba play prominent roles in the paintings I'm about to see, *The Music Lesson* and London's two National Gallery paintings, *A Lady Seated at a Virginal* and *A Lady Standing at a Virginal.* The instruments no longer accompany the subjects; they *are* the subjects, just as in many modernist paintings.

This is perhaps my issue with the later work. I've come to Vermeer primarily for what his paintings teach me about myself, by placing me in the grip of intimacy, of romance, and allowing me to think about my own responses. But the context has changed, and I feel more than a little lost now.

5. Maria

I exit through the front this time, and cross over the steaming, emerald heath again, past Spaniard's Inn, haunt of the Romantics, on my right. When I come to a fork in the road, I turn left down East Heath, rather than back down High Street. It is all village on my right, the backs of the brick rowhouses. The great heath, with its paths and pastures, prams and joggers and leashed dogs, is on my left. I come to Keats's Grove, an island of ghostly sycamores with great, flat leaves, then round the corner to Keats's House. It consists of two white Regency cottages: one belonging to Keats's friend Charles Brown, who took him in when he was ill; the other to the family of his true love, Fanny Brawne. The cottages were later joined to form a single abode. Keats lived here from 1818 to 1820, which means he spent nearly his entire writing life here.

Vermeer is a new love; Keats a first love. I've never been one to make pilgrimages; I don't much care to visit author's homes. The life isn't in the shrine; it's in the work. But because I'm here, I allow myself an hour to traipse through the rooms. It is a comfortable, studiously quiet house, with creaky floorboards. I look at the painting of Keats by Severn in the sitting room. Upstairs, next to Keats's bedroom, is a glass case containing mementoes of his romance with Fanny. I'm riveted by the gold engagement ring that Keats, flat broke and showing the first signs of tuberculosis, gave the lovely eighteen-year-old. The story goes that Fanny never took off the ring, despite her marriage a few years after Keats's death in Rome. I'd always pictured this ring—its gem a lowly garnet stone, all he could afford—as humble, a peasant offering. In fact I find it rather sophisticated, its open scrollwork carved in a beautifully expressive, abstract style. The stone itself is quite worn.

Writing to her, Keats said, "Indeed I think a real Love is enough to occupy the wildest heart . . . "

I walk out into the garden. There's little to see, besides beds of violets and the plum tree beneath which Keats wrote "Ode to a Nightingale." (This tree is a graft from the original tree, actually.) I rummage in the depths of my backpack for my snack, a bruised red pear saved from breakfast at the hotel. I sit on a bench and eat it. Leaving, I turn left toward High Street, the main drag, and Hampstead Station. Remembering how I'd climbed the hill toward Kenwood, I turn left downhill and walk for a block or two, but I don't recognize anything in the dense and cheerful profusion of cafés, flower shops, sundry boutiques.

Out of one of them, a woman suddenly appears, is walking next to me—a beautiful woman about my age in formal black raincoat, ivory scarf. (I'm in my Rockports, jeans, green heather sweater.) Both of us are walking rather quickly downhill, both of us are going somewhere. I make up my mind to catch her with a longer stride or two. "Excuse me, can you tell me where Hampstead Station is?" I ask.

"Where are you trying to go?" she says, without breaking pace. Her voice is low and as indeterminately exotic as her darkly swept-back looks, the clack/clack of her heels on brick.

"London," I say.

She laughs softly, out of the corner of her glance. "This *is* London," she says, with a quick, open wave of a hand encompassing everything.

"I mean, you know, the center. Trafalgar. The National Gallery," I say.

"Hampstead Station is back that way," she says, pointing behind us up the hill. "But you might as well keep going to Belsize Park, it's the same distance either way."

We walk along, through a stoplight, still without breaking stride. The street we are on has changed to Rosslyn Hill.

"Straight ahead," she says. "Are you a Kiwi?"

"What?"

"Are you from New Zealand?"

"No. America. U. S.," I say.

"Oh. What part?"

"North Carolina."

"Hmm, I'm surprised. Most Americans have big voices. Noisy." She smiles, she shrugs. "Yours is soft." After a moment, she adds, "I mean, it's nice. I like it."

"What about you—where are you from?" I ask.

"I'm from Colombia. But I've been here a long time."

Softly, softly, out of the corner of her attention.

Off to the left, the Royal Free Hospital looms above the rolling precincts of lawns and parking lots, fenced tennis courts.

"Your station is another block. Look, you can see the sign," she says. Beyond the next corner, the blocks of trendy cafés and shop fronts begin again, and among them, the sign for the tube—a red "O" with a blue bar across it. Gray-blue ink of evening in the electric air.

She stops at the light. "This is my street," she says.

"My name is Michael."

"Maria."

Another soft smile. She turns left, walks on, doesn't look back. The fragrance in her wake lingers another moment, as cool as irises.

6. Buckingham Palace

When I step out of the Green Park station, it's already dark. Rain is falling hard, umbrellas snapping open the moment each one enters the night. I open mine as well. For a moment, I am not walking somewhere; I am simply moving with the tide. I had picked out this station randomly, because it seemed to be in the middle of the map. Outside, on the corner, stands a treelike black finger post; one of the signs points to "BUCKINGHAM PALACE." I turn right, negotiate a plywood walkway, and find myself on a sidewalk crossing The Green Park. I walk beneath a file of lampposts ghosting among the dappled, white-and-grayish London planes, their leaves the size of notebook paper.

I come out of the park at the Mall, St. James Palace on my left, and the imperial wedding-cake extravaganza of Victoria Memorial a few hundred feet to my right. I turn and walk past the marble queen on her throne—a gilt Victory presiding above her—round the roundabout, toward the façade of Buckingham looming just behind, with its wrought-iron, gilt-topped gates. I veer around to the portico of the Queen's Gallery on the left side, and between the squat Ionic columns guarding the entrance.

"What time do you close?" I ask the man at the counter. He's short and grizzled and reddish, with extremely sharp gray eyes.

"Good evening, sir," he says. "The gallery closes at 17:30. I'm closing this desk now. Would you like to buy a ticket?"

I check my watch: 4:45.

"One more question," I say, smiling, my bankcard out. "Do you happen to have Vermeer's *The Music Lesson* on display?"

"Yes, sir. It's right upstairs. After we go through (he glances toward the walk-through metal detector), I'll take you up." He processes my check card, I sign the receipt, and then he conducts me through and on to the coatroom to check my backpack. "Wait," I say, asking for my pack again. I fish out my notebook and Uniball.

"I'm sorry, sir. No pens in the gallery. Pencil-lead only."

"My problem is, I can't *see* pencil-lead anymore."

He mulls this over for a moment. "Well," he says, "just be prepared to give up the pen if someone asks for it. Shall we go?" We're walking toward the service elevator just beneath the staircase. "It's faster this way." He winks. "You'll have more time with the painting."

In the elevator, he asks, "So you're a writer, eh? Traveling the world, seeing the Vermeers, and writing a book about it, are you?"

This takes me aback. How did he know? He waits for the door to close, then presses the button with a slight smile.

"Yep," I say. I mention my day at Windsor. The erroneous web site.

He nods, with a grin. "Well, it sounds like a brilliant project," he says. "Brilliant."

He holds the glass door leading into the exhibition room open for me. World's best museum staff, I'm thinking.

Then, as we enter the room, I see the painting from twenty-five feet away, say, "Oh Lord," and open my notebook. I say "thank you," as he discreetly takes his leave, bowing faintly, like a trusted lackey in Shakespeare. I glance back, but it's too late: I've missed his name.

7. The Music Lesson

"saturate, intoxicating"   "slaked, immediate"

I write these words in the upper corners of my notebook. The pull of the painting is instantaneous, mesmerizing.

A girl with her back to me is playing the virginal, centered against the far wall. Her suitor stands stock-still in profile to the right, his right forearm propped on the corner of the instrument as he listens intently to the song. From a distance, his face looks affectless, zoned-out. It reminds me a little of the ambiguous face of *Young Woman with Water Pitcher* in New York. I spend several minutes looking at him, trying to decide how I feel. But I keep glancing at the back of the girl's head every few seconds; somehow, more tension is expressed *there* than in the man's face. It's possible to read his disengaged expression as a natural effect of being so entranced by the music, that he is no longer aware of time, or even of his own body. Considering the romantic theme, it would be hard to imagine a more remote existential state than the one this young man seems to be in, even a few feet from his love.

There is a dizzying sense of depth in this painting—it's by far the deepest of Vermeer's interiors. The room is expanded to cathedral-like dimensions; the lovers are lost in the moment, and so am I. The distance from the couple to me—or to the frontal plane of the canvas—is emphasized in a number of ways.

First is the extent of the left wall visible. This elongated wall is a complex scheme which shows, this once, half of the second set of windows—for there would have been three pairs of windows, consisting of upper and lower casements, on the wall of the studio, the third set behind the standpoint and thus out of view. This second casement was the second source of light, responsible for the doubled shadows here, as well as in other paintings. The leading in the windows is the same abstract, circles-and-squares pattern present in seven other Vermeers. The wall gradually lightens toward the back. There is a similarly exaggerated view of the floor, which here appears as white squares (with the artist's characteristic freehand marbling) on a black ground, and this simple pattern practically counts the number of footfalls through the room for us. It's also one of the few Vermeers that reveal the roof-beams, which are beautifully weathered, and aligned across my sight as if, again, to measure the distance between the couple and myself.

In place of the ethereal, sun-raked emptiness of the left-hand side of the painting, the right half is a feast of objects. First, there is the table, covered with the luxurious, crimson-and-blue-on-ochre Persian carpet, its heavy fringe splayed dramatically on the cold marble floor. Atop the table floats a delicate silver platter bearing a white porcelain pitcher that glows like a risen moon. I notice how the platter itself is defined—as simply as the pearl in *Girl with a Pearl Earring*—by an irregular, freehand, platinum line on the sunlit edge. Just behind all that, there's a cerulean blue chair that stands, facing the light, between the table and the couple. I lean in close and see the brilliant, white-gold studs on the chair—the paint laid on so thick that each stud actually protrudes from the canvas, much as real, hammered rivets would protrude from the leather. I reel back for a moment, dazzled.

From a distance, the saturated impression is overwhelming. Many elements of the painting are either bright gold or ochre, especially the virginal at the center, which is both—its raised lid bearing the ornate inscription "Musica Letitiae Comes Medicina Doloris." ("Music, the companion of joy, the balm of sorrow.") The girl, in her creamy yellow blouse, stands before it, and the amber bass viol lies face up behind her, between her back and the viewer. The blue in this room is more covert—the chair is the only overtly blue object. Still, the atmosphere is drenched with lapis, smoldering in the carpet and the shadows, even in the black-blue tiles of the floor. The entire foreground seethes deep blue, like a surreal poem of fire.

This dialogue between Vermeer's favorite colors pervades the entire atmosphere of the room. Portions of the wall and the virginal are either gold with sun, or blue with shadow. The gold bass viol and the bright blue chair beside it await whoever would play or sit. And, looking again at the two windows, I see how the right-hand casement shimmers with golden light, while the one on the left is cool and blue. I think if I could actually see outside, there'd be a building on the right, and nothing but blue sky on the left. But I can't know that, all I know is what the glass contains—the glass that seductively refracts the world rather than revealing it, and in so doing makes it seem new and strange.

And then there is the couple, frozen forever in what appears to be a distant rapture. He is all formal elegance, his tunic black as the hat of the officer in the Frick, as he gazes at her, lost in thought, afloat on the currents of her song. The sun strikes her, as she plays, on her creamy yellow left sleeve. I lean in close and make out the vanishing point, the pinhole in her sleeve, where the rigorous geometry of the room is centered. One thing that makes this painting especially complicated is that there's a mirror, hanging on the wall above the keyboard, reflecting the woman's face, which the viewer could not otherwise see. In the looking-glass world, the woman's gaze is turned toward the man—though her figure below, in our own world, keeps her eyes on her music. Vermeer revised the woman's position, I've read, turning her discreetly away from the man, and yet he took the liberty of leaving her reflection as it was, stealing a mysterious glance.

It is a circular, closed system of glances, like that of *The Art of Painting,* and the viewer is part of the system—we are complicit, privy to secrets. In the same way that one seems to glimpse, by chance, the model's image being painted on the canvas in *The Art of Painting,* just so I catch the girl's reflection in the mirror here, in *The Music Lesson.* There is also a famous enigma in this mirror, above the face of the woman: one can see the leg of an easel, and just beyond that, part of a box presumed to contain the artist's supplies. The easel would have been located in the center of the room, of course, where the artist (and the viewer) would stand. In other words, he puts himself, for once, smack into the intensely private orbit of the scene. A self-reflexive gesture? A calculated tease? But why?

The view is as simplistic, yet charged with as much meaning as the inscription itself, or the precious pitcher, or the visible part of a painting hanging to the right behind them—a popular and rather lascivious genre scene known as a *Roman Charity.* A father, Cimon, who has been condemned to starve in chains, is secretly breastfed by his daughter, Pero. I don't know how that twisted drama, with its shades of pathos and eros, relates to Vermeer's scene of extraordinary refinement, but I think it refers to the "balm" of music in the context of love's captivity.

Vermeer, in fact, is sometimes described as "voyeuristic"—a word that conflicts jarringly with his sensitivity. His modern parallel is Degas: both specialized in the anatomies of intimate, unguarded moments. I imagine Vermeer crouching in his darkened booth, examining every square centimeter. I wonder if the impulse to paint some part of himself into the picture this time was a matter of naturalism, a way of acknowledging the inescapable fact of his own existence. A way, perhaps, of dispelling part of the voyeuristic shadow he must have felt he cast on his work. In any case, it's as close as we get to a self-portrait—this nebulous bit of easel.

I check my watch: *5:15*. No one has entered the room. I can only see this painting for the first time once. I understand that what I am doing—trying to memorize every existing detail—is hopeless. And yet there's something sacred here, and I want to burn it into memory. Fifteen minutes left. I stand up.

I'm remembering something that I'd seen on leaving Kenwood a couple of hours ago. I'd crossed in front of the seemingly endless length of the stuccoed mansion to the other end, where the drive led out and away. On my left, the magnificent grounds swooped down toward some enchanted forest from childhood. There in the distance, a three-arched, white wooden footbridge stood at the edge of the clearing, nestled among the oaks, the meadows lit with daffodils.

But the bridge that completes the picture isn't a real bridge. It's a folly, a flat apparition called The Sham Bridge that, when viewed from the right distance and against the pastoral backdrop of Hampstead Heath, can't help but succeed. Even though I already knew all of this—because I'd read about it in a guidebook—I still half believed in the bridge when I walked past it.

Vermeer fits comfortably into this illusionist tradition, along with artists like Fabritius and van Hoogstraten. But the Vermeer paintings that foreground such trickery, works like *The Little Street* or *The Love Letter*, are anomalies. It's more common for Vermeer to use his magic sparingly and selectively. The plump ruff of a jacket, the sheen of a pearl or a lower lip are precise and irresistible appeals. They are servants of the painting's cause.

Then I look at the suitor here: his figure evanescent, thinly painted, with an evanescent, even more thinly painted sash across his chest. He's nearly a see-through man, a lost ghost, as transparent as his sash. In the optical scheme, the objects in the middle distance are in hard focus; those toward the back, like the man, the inscription, the painting-within-the-painting, are not.

5:28. I notice how the handle on the pitcher is turned to the right, as if offering itself to the grasp—to my grasp, though, not to either of the figures behind it. It is a satisfyingly substantial, broadly curved handle, sunlit on its inside edge. Easy to imagine its heft in the hand. The brilliant blue chair faces me; the neck of the bass viol beside it lies comfortably close; and the scalloped sides of the viol's body are perfectly made to be held between the thighs.

With all this, I don't need to see the man clearly—I feel the song for myself.

The door opens behind me. It's a different guard, a woman this time, to tell me that the museum is closing. I nod and jot:

didn't get very far—

then I turn my back, a difficult thing to do, on *The Music Lesson.*

8. Faux

As I join the guard in the doorway, I half-whisper, trying to keep my voice down, "What a lovely room this is." I gesture vaguely behind me at its green linen-covered walls; elaborate zigzag hardwood parquet; and arched central skylight, with flanking glass panels embellished with enormous plaster flowers.

"Yes, well . . . it isn't what it seems," she says in a normal speaking voice, because we're the last ones left in the building.

"What do you mean?"

She stops and turns. She's ageless, a sparkling, pale-eyed red-head in a royal-blue uniform with scarlet trim. Her gold nametag reads: "Diane."

"Well, these walls for instance. Here. Try this," she says, stepping back into the room and rapping sharply with her knuckles. "See?"

I rap: it is a fake wall, a movable soundproof partition.

"But . . ." I say, looking at the marble baseboards.

"Plastic," she says, with a twinkle. I lean over and rap there as well.

"Look at the size of some of these canvases. How do you think we fit them in through these doors?" She pauses. "We don't. We build the room around them."

I ask her about the skylight, the flowers. She tells me they were recently cast from antique molds discovered in the palace basement after the war. Then she leads me out onto the landing, raps on the greenish marble columns flanking the marble stairs: hollow tin. But skillfully painted tin. It passes. Diane points out how some of these doors, with inset windows, lead into galleries; in other doors, the insets are filled with mirrors. She takes out her keys, unlocks one of these doors so I can see how each doorway is equipped with the foldable mirror behind it. Depending on the exhibition, each door can be used as a door or camouflaged as a mirrored partition that seems to enlarge the room.

"Look," she says. "We're especially proud of this."

She places her palm on the deeply burnished mahogany hand-rail, set atop black wrought iron balusters. Beneath the rail, a length of bright-gold tasseled rope loops among and around each baluster, and so on down the steps. I touch the velvet rope only to discover it too is cold wrought iron—shockingly cold—that was forged and painted to look exactly, drape exactly like heavy braided rope, woven sinuously through the more literal wrought iron balusters.

"Yes," she says. "It's faux. It's real faux." She beams. Then walks me cheerfully, conspiratorially even, down to the locked entrance, her keys jangling at her waist.

It's only a taste of mystery, this hour like the tick of rain on glass—and it leaves me a little unsteady on my feet.

9. Lightness

I walk back to my hotel through damp streets shining with moonlight, past the ghost-white swans afloat in St. James Park, thinking about the see-through man in *The Music Lesson*. From a certain distance, he is Vermeer's way of expressing the lightness of love.

Marriage, I'm thinking, is often the opposite. For instance, the summer when Sophia was one, we took a celebratory trip through Germany and Italy. For the first part of it, Sara was singing with the university choir, in various village churches in Bavaria. For weeks, I carried a wonderfully heavy sleepy baby on my back, along with a diaper bag on my arm, as I manhandled two huge, tweed suitcases onto and off of crowded buses and sweltering regional trains, through countless inns and hostels and customs offices. The fancy, wheeled suitcases were Swiss—they weren't Swiss-made, but they had a catchy Swiss brand name that eludes me now, with an embroidered Swiss red cross for a logo. They were stuffed with gifts for everyone Sara could think of, and the suitcases themselves were gifts to us, purchased in honor of our rediscovered marital happiness in one of those flowery riverboat towns along the Rhine. The suitcases would never be used again after this summer. I remember wheeling and slinging and hoisting my comically heavy burden through the pristine train stations of Germany and Switzerland, through the gloriously grimy and chaotic stations of Italy. I took pride in the sheer athleticism of this feat; few could have managed it. I also took pride in my gifted wife and angelic blonde baby girl. I felt nearly invincible then, though the marriage was in its last months.

Perhaps the lightness exists only in falling in love. The summer after my ninth grade year was the summer of my first love. I was living with my father on Wilson Avenue in Columbia, in the first of a series of rather unfortunate houses he rented for us. One day

I discovered Hinkson Creek through thick bushes at the end of the narrow, brick street. After that, I was always heading off down there—the cool and sheltered feel of it big enough to lose myself in for a day.

Walking home one evening, a voice called out to me, a mellow and matter-of-fact girl's voice called out to me from a porch swing as I passed. I think I waved and kept my head down, unsure if I'd imagined it. But on my way home the very next day, I gathered my nerve when I saw her again. She called, *Hello there, hello again*, and I stopped.

Her name was Cheryl. She lived in New Jersey, but was visiting her grandmother in Columbia that summer. She stands slim and gracefully tall in memory; but in reality, she was an inch shorter than I was then. Similarly, she seems forever wise to me, because she had already turned sixteen, while I was still fifteen. Dusk after dusk, we sat on that swing together, drinking orange or grape soda, watching the butterflies waft down the street in shafts of green-gold light. Here was something I knew about, and could explain to her: their names, Monarchs and Viceroys and Cabbage Moths, and the differences between them. Slowly each sunset sank—those lush, flamingo sunsets of the Midwest. Bats jittered amongst the trees, and fireflies soundlessly lit up one by one a few feet above each lawn. I couldn't believe her green-eyed prettiness: fine freckles and eyebrows and perfectly tilted nose. I couldn't believe the fact of her sitting so peacefully, merely an inch away from me.

This was the closest I've been to *The Music Lesson's* dreamy sensation of romance, its almost narcotic suspension of time and place. It wouldn't have occurred to me to ask her to go anywhere, to want for anything more than what each moment already provided. We didn't talk much. When we did, we imagined careers, or told our dreams, or wished on the first star, that sort of thing. Sometime after dark, her grandmother would call her in, and I'd drift home in a state of profound disequilibrium.

I can say she was exactly one inch shorter than I because of our first kiss, which took place on her darkened porch, where dead June bugs lay on their backs along the edges and beneath the swing, too many to ever sweep away. It was ten p.m.; it was time for me to go. "Well," she said, and then I rose, and she rose too, and immediately took me by the elbows. I didn't let on I'd never kissed anyone before, had never even been that close to a girl before. We were standing almost nose to nose, after weeks of maintaining a calculated distance, after weeks when the only touch allowed was an incidental brush of wrist or shoulder, after weeks when my entire nervous system, root and capillary, ached with an almost painful electromagnetic current.

She stood on tiptoe, and I leaned this way, and she leaned that way and lifted her mouth to mine, and then I kissed her, tasted her lip-gloss and grape soda, flickering tip of her tongue, her half-closed, spangled irises a fraction of an inch from mine. All this while, she seemed to keep shifting maddeningly back and forth in my arms, like weather I thought, like glimpses of some fabulous landscape I was traveling through that kept unfolding at every turn. That's when I learned what heaven is: proximity.

10. Alice

It's Sunday, my last day in London. On the enormous black-and-white marble portico in front of the National Gallery, I'm leaning—palms splayed against the iron railing, set between Corinthian columns—into the view, the moment. It would be a perfect smoke break if I still smoked, like the black-haired kid in his Levi jacket a couple of columns away from me. Ashen rainclouds hover over London. Nelson's Column presides above Trafalgar Square, with four colossal brass lions at the base of each corner, and a fountain on each side of it with lyrically plumbed dolphins, mermaids, and tritons. The double-deckers queue and pull over, colors like cigarette embers. On my left, the high plinth of St. Martin-in-the-Fields. The white facades, gilt lettering of Canada House, South Africa House flank the square.

"Pardon me, sir, no smoking on the portico," a guard who has come out from inside says to the youth. She gleams in her slim navy suit; she seems Indian or Pakistani. She suggests he go down to the square.

"Okay, sorry," he says, and heads for the steps. "Sorry."

I watch her stride elegantly back across the checkerboard mosaic floor of the portico—across the seven rows of black marble squares, laid on a bias, to the front door. I'm reminded of something in *Alice in Wonderland*, of how Alice finds her way across the enormous chessboard, crossing from square to square—though she herself does not always seem to be aware of it—because of the borders of asterisks, three staggered rows that the eye leaps over before resuming reading:

*　　*　　*　　*
　*　　*　　*
*　　*　　*　　*

When Sophia sees the asterisks, she says, "*Look*—we're crossing over!" wriggling in my lap. There's a brief, held-breath sensation of flight. And then the story takes off again.

The point of the chess game was to create what Carroll called "a dream of a pawn's-eye view of a looking-glass game of chess." I'm thinking of Vermeer like that. What he paints is a pawn's eye view of love—as far as love can even be seen, as far as love can ever be known by chalk line, lens, and north light slanting into a room.

11. The Sphinx

Inside the National Gallery, I climb the stairs—two flights, two touches of the brass rail at my right hand—then turn left at the top. I have all afternoon. I pass through several long, cool galleries, searching for Room 16—which, according to my museum map, is where I'll find the two Vermeers that have always seemed to belong here, at the end of my travels. I look for the room number where I am: it's 23.

Directly in front of me is Rembrandt's rough-hewn, ravishing *Woman Bathing in a Stream* (1654) referencing Susanna and her story, and then his 1669 *Self Portrait at the Age of 63,* one of the last of the line, the pursed, collapsed intelligence gathered, as usual, by focused chiaroscuro about the sagging and spectral eyes. On the opposite wall is Carel Fabritius' powerful self-portrait entitled *Young Man in a Fur Cap,* from 1654, the year he died. The steel breastplate he's wearing, with its heavy impasto sun-glint, is exactly the type of archaic embellishment Rembrandt often added. It reminds me also of the outlandish turban in *Girl with a Pearl Earring.* Something that all three painters share is a devastating frankness, a kind of naturalism that is, interestingly, complemented by such exotic costumes.

There could have been no Vermeer without his mentor, Fabritius. I pull my notebook out of my backpack, jot down the titles, a bit of description about each ("level gaze," "luminosity" and so forth), and then head onward.

The long galleries end; the more intimate scale of each room ahead signals to me that I'm close to where Vermeer will be. An odd apparatus dominates the center of Room 17, which is filled with miniatures by Leiden painters including Gerrit Dou and Roland Savery. This cumbersome apparatus is Samuel Van Hoogstraten's perfectly preserved "peepshow." It's the only survivor among many, a big wooden perspective box (c. 1655–60) with a decorated exterior, on a wooden pedestal. One side is open to admit light; there's an aperture to "peep" through on each of the narrower ends.

Leaning down and peering inside is unsettling, as the complete interior of a Dutch house unfolds in anamorphic perspective, with all sorts of trompe-l'oeil doorways, paintings-within-the-paintings, mirrors, even a trusty black-and-white dog sitting in the center of the black-and-white floor. Hoogstraten's signature is found in the deliciously clever form of a self-addressed letter lying casually on the seat of a chair. As a whole, the box is simply an illusionist masterpiece, its hues and textures as saturated and intense and magical as a Vermeer.

Now I see how much of what we believe about Vermeer—"The Sphinx of Delft," as the nineteenth century French critic Thoré-Bürger named him, casting him as an enigmatic genius—is wrong.

Vermeer was never alone. The vocabulary that we associate with him—the geometrical patterns of the tiled floors, the straight-backed, leather-upholstered chairs, the treatment of glass, even the meticulously measured rake of light though space—is here, too, in this box, as clearly as in Vermeer's paintings. Suddenly I know how Alice must have felt—after finding the correct minia-ture door for her miniature key—on peering through the tunnel "not much larger than a rat-hole" into the "loveliest garden you ever saw."

I straighten up, as dizzy as seventeenth-century viewers must have felt when peering for the first time into these depths. I feel an instinct to write something, and unfold my notebook on the top of the priceless cabinet unthinkingly, but a guard appears out of nowhere to say, "It's not a desk, sir."

Yes. I'm sorry. "I'm sorry."

12. A Lady Standing at a Virginal

Room 16 is intimate, the size of my living room, and exquisitely curated, with the two Vermeers on the right as I go in. A guard is posted in a chair in the doorway. There's a wooden settee in the center of the room—the kind that flexes comfortably in the mid-dle—still close enough to view the Vermeers quite well.

They are arranged on a wall, alternating with paintings of church interiors by Dutch architectural painters, two by Pieter Saanredam and a third by Emanuel de Witte. It seems a little jarring at first to have the Vermeer women framed by paintings of churches. A spiritual statement of some sort? An homage to the homeland? I realize a couple of things, though. There's more than a little com-mon ground between Vermeer and the architectural tradition, with its quasi-scientific study of light, its rigorous design. I decide I like seeing Vermeer's whitewashed walls beside Saanredam's ascetic Calvinist spaces.

On the other three walls are Dutch genre paintings—including a bawdy drinking scene by Gabriel Metsu, entitled *Two Men with a*

Sleeping Woman (c. 1655–69) and Pieter De Hooch's sunny master-piece *The Courtyard of a House In Delft* (1658).

Now it's pretty clear to me why the curator has hung these particular paintings—these genre scenes, as well as the church interiors—in support of *A Lady Standing at a Virginal* and *A Lady Seated at a Virginal*. It's because they show us the context, the cul-ture—both sacred and profane—that produced Vermeer.

One question that lingers over Vermeer's two ladies is whether or not they were intended as pendants. Pendants would typically be a married couple, but elaborations on a subject, as these ladies appear to be, were also a popular type of pendant. Both paintings are studies of a woman staring provocatively into the viewer's eyes and posed with an instrument—and it's the same instrument and the same room, and the paintings themselves are almost exactly the same size. Whether they were conceived as pendants or not, it was only in 1910 that they were permanently reunited here, and have since set up shop as a pair.

I take off my green wool sweater, wrap the sleeves around my waist and tie them there. I slide my backpack under the bench—the guard watches but doesn't object—and move to about eight feet in front of *A Lady Standing at a Virginal*. I check my watch. I stare for about twenty minutes, then retrieve my notebook, and try to record my thoughts.

More than any other Vermeer, I feel, this one memorializes. A tall, young woman, dressed very formally, stands with stiff spine, hands disappearing mysteriously into the recess of the keyboard on the right. Her benign, familiar smile is tinged with a greenish shadow. The eye tracks into the center from an extraordinarily luminous casement. The painting is evenly lit, pale gold, subdued, except for the lavish brilliance in this window, whose leading is del-icate, formal, simple. There is no drama in this window, as in the windows of most Vermeers—as in the dingy, workaday window in *The Milkmaid,* for instance, or the crisp, abstract mosaic of the window in *Young Woman with a Water Pitcher.* The light falls on the woman's face, but this time, we're not rewarded with an angelic vision, as we are in *The Milkmaid*, but with what seems a deliberately darkened face. This puzzles me, and I want to linger, but my eye is drawn to the back wall of the room, where three paintings are displayed in close succession.

First, there's an extraordinarily ornate gilt frame containing a pastoral landscape. I note the rapid, abstract gold-on-gold brushwork of the frame, which lends an illusion of fine detail. Then, in the center of the wall, above the woman's head, hangs a considerably larger painting of Cupid in an ebony frame. Finally, another landscape painting adorns the underside of the keyboard's lid; such decoration was common. This painting faces from the right of the room back toward the woman and the window. In a clever twist of scholarship, Gregor Weber has shown that the two landscape paintings are in reality versions of the same actual painting, *Mountain Landscape with Travelers*, by the Delft painter Pieter Groenewegen. Though it's common for maps and paintings to reappear in different paintings, to include the same painting-within-a-painting *twice* in this particular composition seems remarkable to me.

The vanishing point, the pinprick in *A Lady Standing at a Virginal* is centered on her heart. There's an eerie symmetry to the room—the lower casement and the instrument's painted landscape facing each other directly, through the young woman's torso. She stands stock-still at the center of an extraordinarily well-defined space. Nothing is concealed; nothing is left to chance.

My eye moves on to the plump, golden Cupid on the back wall. This is the third appearance of Cesar van Everdingen's Cupid—completing the series begun with *A Maid Asleep,* where only the left foot is visible, and continuing with *Girl Interrupted in Her Music.* It's as if it were planned, this gradual revelation. But how could Vermeer have foreseen what would come?

In any case, this Cupid takes the place that another figure might have taken in a painting like *Officer and Laughing Girl.* He stands slightly to the lady's right—his bow, as he leans against it, planted firmly as if on the top of her head. He becomes her, she becomes him, and the message, the romantic theme, isn't lost on me.

And so she looks out at me through the picture's plane—near the end of the glances, the series of Cupids, near the end of my journey through Vermeer. I've read that the unusual greenish hue of her shadowed face is due to the Italian Renaissance practice of using a green underpainting to neutralize the pink skin tones on the surface. She's a little matronly, with a prominent nose—and if her gaze is inviting at all, it's hard to tell, because her face is small and doll-like. The greenish shadow is very noticeable; it's difficult to find her appealing, at least in any conventional way.

Still, the painting insists on presenting the lady as a beauty, an object of desire. Many details of the painting sing praises to her—the lascivious little cupid speaking openly (at last) on her behalf; her elaborate formal hairdo, with beaded chignon and delicate ringlets hanging across her forehead; and the elaborate formal silk gown with scarlet bows tied in front of her bodice. Also, her elegant *tabbaard* would seem to celebrate marriage. Her eyes are matter-of-fact, expectant and unsurprised by my presence in the room. She's waiting calmly for me to take my seat—on the inviting expanse of the cerulean velvet cushion on the chair, while the brass rivets gleam along the seatback, precious as pearls. We're used to each other by now, in the assumed intimacy the painting projects, and she doesn't shock, or draw me toward some agonizing and self-aware precipice.

This painting has a completely different kind of intensity from that of *The Milkmaid* or *Woman Holding a Balance.* Here, the red ribbons leap as much from the contrast with the coolness of her blue bodice and shadowed face, from the scarcity of warmth, as from any quality of their own. The wall glows with a pristine, other-worldly evenness. I sit on the bench; I move in to look for half-hour intervals. Hard to believe such softness of line, such spectral shapes dissolving in the gaze.

Close up, I notice that the frame of the cupid painting casts a triangular sliver of shadow beside it on the wall. Because the painting leans outward on its nail, this shadow points down. It's actually composed of two separate triangles—one darker than the other, similar to the doubled shadows in *The Music Lesson.* This late in my journey I've a special fondness for such small, yet effective illusion-ist tricks, and the sense of space they create.

A guard asks, "Is this your backpack?" Asks me twice, before I understand what he's talking about—*yes,* I nod, as I gather my stuff from the floor.

Actually, I hadn't noticed the doubled shadows at first. The patterns of light and shade are too "natural" to make much of an impression. It's a phenomenon we deal with unconsciously, on a retinal level. In the case of the famous earring, for instance, the eye takes in two brushstrokes—and we fill in the rest unaware.

Against this brightly lit wall, Vermeer assembles his great poem of shadows. There's a row of characteristic Delftware tiles along the baseboards, each white square with a single, blue figure—a cupid fishing, for instance—little scenes that seem to reflect on the subject of romance. My eye moves from tile to tile as if following a trail of clues. Then I study the black-and-white marble floor—with cloudy, stylized veins in the white tiles. It seems to me his most carefully measured floor, his most carefully measured cube of space.

"Look! A Vermeer!" says a visitor. With a bustle of umbrellas, several pass: wet over-clothes and squeaky shoes.

It still seems odd that this woman—part lady, part love god-dess—regards me with such a shadowed, greenish face. And yet everything that might ordinarily attract my eye in this luminous painting is similarly shadowed: her mouth, her chest, her arms and hands, even the pearls at her throat dissolve to a smoky blur.

I look into her face for fifteen minutes or so, then look away. Then try again. After the intensities of *The Milkmaid,* of *The Girl with a Pearl Earring,* and all the others, this small and enigmatic face seems almost disinterested in me. But the longer I look, the more I trust her, and the more placid she appears, at ease in her clothes, in this light, in this room. As tall as she is, she floats in space—and gazes slightly down on me—and would appear even taller if I took the seat.

I imagine sitting two feet from her silk dress, with its lovely, columnar shadows, my right shoulder nearly touching the upper left corner of the side of the virginal—where, I've read, the artist has signed the work, though I've never seen the signature because it isn't visible in the reproductions. I lean in close now, reading glasses on, and find it—faint as it is, his monogram "Meer" with the letter *I* inserted in the *V* of the *M*.

This isn't one of Vermeer's more popular paintings. But for the moment—seeing and being seen by the lady—the image feels ennobling, and I feel worthy of it.

13. A Lady Seated at a Virginal

I've moved a few feet to the right, and taken up a comfortable viewpoint, Uniball in hand. I write, "questionable morals." This is my immediate response to the sly, come-hither glance of *A Lady Seated at a Virginal*. In *A Lady Standing,* the virginal is on the right and the woman faces right. In *A Lady Seated,* the virginal is on the left and the woman faces left. The scenarios are opposite, and so is my response. Rather than standing back contemplatively, as I did with *A Lady Standing,* I'm drawn in close to this slouching woman. Her expression is coyly neutral from a distance, but up close she seems to flash a knowing smile—almost a leer.

There is a floral curtain hanging at the upper left foreground, similar to that in *The Art of Painting* and *Allegory of Faith*. The curtain not only adds depth in this scene, but also a sense of voyeuristic pleasure to the ambiguous scene beyond it, in the room. Especially striking is the strangely phosphorescent glow of the Delftware baseboard tiles in the shadows beneath the virginal. The out-of-focus figures in each tile swim through the darkness like miniature, deep-sea creatures. Propped in the foreground is the startlingly crisp, whisky-colored viola de gamba, each of its six strings molten and clear. How odd it is that this instrument is the only clearly focused object in the room!

Some regard this painting as Vermeer's last work, in part because it seems to fulfill a certain trajectory. Wheelock wrote that "his brushwork became more abstract" as he matured, and lists *A Lady*

Seated at a Virginal as an example of this. The lack of focus here has led some to insinuate that Vermeer's art was beginning to decline due to the circumstances (poverty, despair, perhaps even madness) that would soon lead to his death. 1672 is known as the *Rampjaar,* the Dutch "disaster year," when France and England invaded the United Provinces, and the great economy collapsed. *A Lady Seated at a Virginal* is a product of the *Rampjaar.*

Wheelock also says that "none of the nuances of human psychology in his earlier works are present here." I'm not sure I'd go that far, but the difference from earlier works is glaring. Take, for instance, the painting-within-a-painting. It's based on a ribald bordello painting called *The Procuress,* that was owned by Vermeer's mother-in-law and has appeared before, in his painting *The Concert.* Here, it is starkly simplified—the three characters (whore, gallant, procuress) almost a cartoon. The gilt frame of the painting, especially the treatment of gold-on-gold highlights, has evolved into a rather listless, abstract pattern of paint daubs.

The window, principal beauty of so many luminous Vermeers, looms like a vestigial afterthought in the darkened corner. It's covered with an indifferently painted blue curtain (the only one like it in the oeuvre), and what we can see of the lower pane reveals only blackness. Is it a night scene? And why include the window at all, only to cover it? The sheet of music, propped on the virginal before the woman, is totally illegible as musical staves, the bars reduced to watery daubs that bleed across the sepia page. And the woman's blue satin dress is hardly more than a jumble of shimmery folds piled up haphazardly on the chair-back behind her. The wall-tiles, so crystalline and convincing in the companion painting, are faded and blurred here. From the painter of precisely scaled maps, of decisively real bricks and stoneware and leaded glass, of the triumphantly palpable weft of the silk dress in *A Lady Standing at a Virginal,* these qualities are disturbing.

One thing especially bothers me. The sidelong rake of light from the left that animates the essence of Vermeer, that *is* Vermeer, is not here. But there is some light falling into the scene, rather than across it. I figure this is related to the second light source, apparently falling from over my left shoulder. The lighting in the pair is another opposite: that which is lit here, remains dark in the other; that which is dark here, is well lit in the other. The face of *A Lady Seated,* as it turns, offers its glowing, doe-eyed prettiness, the fine ringlets about her brow rendered as summary light-strokes. Probably the brightest passage is her pale gold sleeve, dissolving in incandescence.

As for the mute, inviting figure of the viol de gamba, propped majestically in the foreground, it seems to parallel the chair in the other painting. Both objects loom close to the plane of the canvas and work to create depth as well as functioning as stand-ins for the male, situated just where the lover should be, with whom the viewer is aligned. Especially striking is the bow, thrust dramatically through the strings, the grip end angling up to be seen or grasped. Then I notice the brass frets on the fingerboard of the instrument. Actually, I can't really make out the frets themselves, only the blunt ends of each one, where they catch the light, ambiguously smoldering in the dimness. Why is this so moving to me? I suddenly wonder. Then I know. It's as if all the bittersweet erotic energy of one's midlife were concentrated *there,* at my fingertips.

I'm sitting frequently now, weary of marble. (I've been standing on the sides of my aching feet, like a tree sloth.) The guard nods: fifteen minutes. Still, I wonder. Is this painting about sex? I keep returning to certain upright shapes—the bow standing in quivering focus, the stout leg of the virginal—in combination with the woman's own malleable, knowing regard. Seductive, beckoning, subaqueous, the source of the light, here at the end, blanked out beneath blue cloth.

14. The Last Word

I turn back to the standing and seated women. These two figures brood over Vermeer's entire oeuvre: the mistress and the maid. In the earlier work, *A Lady Standing at a Virginal,* the room is bathed in a daunting clarity. Immaculate, soft shadows blend into the luminous white. The cupid stands quite openly at last, announcing the theme of committed love. The woman's benign uprightness confirms it. There's something ceremonious about her stance, about the way her fingers hover limply over the keyboard. It is an undisguised pose, a pause in the midst of her real life with the viewer, her husband. With me.

The invitation in *A Lady Seated at a Virginal* is very different, but equally challenging. Of course, the lady isn't really playing the virginal, which one wouldn't play sitting down in any case. She's simply posing with it—her soft, silky forearms on display— while simultaneously twisting in her seat to meet my gaze. Her lap swivels toward me even as her knees remain at home beneath the keyboard. Her shoulders are slumped, as if she were near-sighted and couldn't see anything very clearly. Her amazingly sinuous, swanlike neck is bent coyly forward, embellished with a lustrous strand of pearls. The only decisive features about her are her onyx irises. The eyes themselves are slightly provocative and almond-shaped. She keeps inviting me, *Come on*, her lips so plump as she turns toward me.

And as I take my leave, I think of the other women, too—the maid at her faux nap, the solitaries, and the letter-readers. The gold-weigher, the lacemaker, the milkmaid. The scumbled flesh tones and shadows of each face. The yearning depths of an earthenware jug, the triumphant sunlit bell tower; every form of love, I imagine, the painter had ever known.

Here at the end, in his pair of ladies at the virginals, Vermeer offers an anatomy of love, both virtuous and carnal. In each, I sit virtually at the lady's lap, and there's nothing subtle about the way I'm addressed. The cupid's inclusion, in *A Lady Standing,* is as clear as day for once, and the woman's figure looms ramrod straight, with her decorous ribbons, her fluted Doric skirt. The cupid here is one of those miracles of simplicity—like looking back, across the Kolk, at one's own life—to see the lineaments of love, the Petrarchan ideal, attached to this matronly woman. Her modest smile, her calm regard is the music she doesn't play. Her beauty is in that manner, in that certainty, that loving acceptance. She sees the best in me. She's what I need, if not always what I want.

In *A Lady Seated,* I'm drawn into the shadowy room almost directly from behind the girl. The procuress on the wall is murky and vague in this case—simplified to its essence—and the girl's figure also displays no will of her own, it seems, except for the will to pose. Truthfully, my instinct is to reach for her. Her dress is a mess of abstraction, and it's a mess because that's how she's sitting, and because that's just the sort of girl she is. It's almost as if she were wearing a daringly open black raincoat, holding a custard pie. It's part of the design, I'd say, part of the work's designs on me. She keeps me honest, too, for no account of love would be complete without her, and her frank acknowledgment. I take another step toward her. The pearls on her throat burn exquisitely, like pinpricks mapping the shadows. She's what I cannot help but want, she's what I can't shake off, she's Vermeer's last word on the matter.

15. Salvation and Shipwreck

Now the guard coughs . . . now he says, "It's time."

I sling my backpack over my shoulder, doggedly scribbling a few last lines in my notebook. Finally, I turn to go.

Down a long corridor, I come to the deserted staircase hall—an immense openness beneath the central glass dome ceiling—and descend, my left fingertips grazing the brass rail, polished gold by human touch. The women hover in my head on the plane between past and future. I remember the twin gates, of ivory and of horn, from Book VI of *The Aeneid*:

> Two gates the silent house of Sleep adorn:
> Of polished ivory this, that of transparent horn:
> True visions through transparent horn arise,
> Through polished ivory pass deluding lies.
> (ll. 893–896. Trans. John Dryden)

I'm the last one out again. My mind is floating a few steps ahead of me, down the marble staircase, past the desk to the right of the entrance, where the Indian girl sits, head down, sorting a pile of audio guides into the various languages. Then I will pass quietly through the slab-glass front door, out through the echoing portico into the watery neon buzz of the square. These two women—salvation and shipwreck—will attend me through the West End theatre marquee throngs: the black umbrellas, drinkers and diners glancing out at me through rainy windows. Past corner pubs all advertising "Sunday Roast" on their chalkboards: savory aromas of minted lamb and beef on the bone and Yorkshire puddings wafting down the sidewalks.

Two Marriages

1. Jackie

If someone could see straight into you, could take in all of you in a single glance, what would he or she see?

I was twenty-eight when I met Jackie, a playwright/director/ actress. She was thirty-seven, a twice-divorced and disillusioned high-school teacher. We were both natives of Columbia, we met, somewhat oddly, in Steamboat Springs, Colorado, at a rustic summer school for performing arts. I was the soft-spoken, newly sober maintenance man; she was the rather flamboyant theatre director, older than I by a decade. She was slim and worldly and wore feathered hats. We charmed and mauled each other for weeks. Then, to our mutual surprise, we discovered we wanted each other for good. What followed was a deliriously happy, seven-year period of growth—during which we both finished doctorates (in Theatre and English) from the University of Utah, and came into our own.

Later, in the late 1980s, at her peak, Jackie got sick and never really got better. She felt cold and nauseated—as if with an endless flu—and lost weight she couldn't afford to lose. Her darkly exotic skin took on an almost jaundiced pallor. Meanwhile, her career was taking off, with endless roles, performances in avant-garde black box productions, as well as in mainstream plays and musicals. She even published a little: poems and plays and critical essays.

She had a summer fellowship in '89 to study at Stratford. She came back gaunt, her complexion positively anemic. This was serious, and she was frightened, but not especially open to advice. By December, it turned out that the fibroid lump in her breast—which had already been thoroughly checked and biopsied and declared benign the previous year—was not, in fact, benign. Back then, "the big C" still seemed the darkest curse of all, and it had taken precious months for her, for me, for everyone to see through the stigma, the secrecy, and the misinformation.

No one who knew her was surprised at how determinedly Jackie fought for her life, through the mastectomies, the latest chemo-cocktails, radiation, and the attempted bone marrow transplant. Every week there was some new, desperate battle to defend the vital centers against an enemy that seemed almost demonic. Which are the dangerous tumors, you wonder; which can you afford to ignore? You don't know, no one knows, but for every tumor she managed to beat back, a couple of new ones appeared, virtually overnight.

After the first round of chemo, the cancer went into remission, and Jackie landed a tenure-track job at the University of Texas. (She was virtually bald at her interview, but carried it off with Sinead O'Connor aplomb.) So we'd parted temporarily—she to Austin, I remaining in Salt Lake, to study for my doctoral exams. Six months later, she was still working her way through the hellish yet optimistic process of breast reconstruction—having her pectoral muscles expanded gradually, one side at a time, over implants filled with salt water—when, in what seemed a malicious irony, the cancer came back. I left Utah immediately, in a U-Haul truck; and though I continued to teach part-time in community colleges here and there, I essentially stayed at her side for the next two years.

The first year together in Austin was the trial of our lives, both of us making great efforts to keep up our careers. Meanwhile, we were trying not to panic, living in hospital wards, arranging trips to places like M.D. Anderson in Houston, and of course, continually convalescing, waiting for blood counts to rebound from the latest chemo or radiation. A fine balance is needed, we learned, as we tried to gauge how aggressively to attack, to try to overwhelm each tumor, while the cancer was aggressively attacking at the same time. And worse than the treatments were the side effects—the gauntlet of fevers, nausea, ulcers, and despair.

But there was happiness all along the way, too. One afternoon, lying in bed in her lovely penthouse apartment in downtown Austin,

I asked if she remembered how we used to talk, in our first years, about getting married. *Why didn't we?* I wondered aloud. A moment later, surprising myself, I asked her, this time for real. Immediately, she said yes—and for a long time, we simply wept quietly and happily. It was our impossibly romantic gift to each other.

A couple of days later, we got dressed up—I wore my one blue suit; she wore a silk dress printed with orchids—and then slipped away to see the judge. We hadn't yet told her parents: we eloped! Jackie was very frail, already walking with a cane, and she had less than a year to live. The room was filled with the purest, most hallowed love imaginable. Our triumph wrested from despair, her hand trembling when I fitted the simple gold ring upon her finger.

Soon enough, it was time for her to resign, for us to go back to Missouri, so that she could be close to her family. We rented a townhouse just up the street from her parents. It wasn't that we had given up, we thought; we were circling our wagons for the real fight. But I remember bathing her one night, a few months before the end, and as I soaped her back, I could feel a bed of new tumors nestled among her ribs and shoulder blades, like walnuts pushing out from beneath her skin. I couldn't count them, and didn't try. I decided not to mention them; her spirits were not often high, and she enjoyed her baths.

Much of Jackie's last year was fogged. She wore a portable morphine pump that delivered doses of morphine through a central line straight into her heart. This contained her pain, but the side effects were grave, and—endlessly generous and brilliant and vivacious as she naturally was—it took everything I had to negotiate the disorientation, paranoia, and hallucinatory rages that so often consumed her now. Even so, we were never closer, never more selflessly, light-heartedly in love than we were in those last six months. We'd been together eight years then—we knew how to comfort each other, crack each other up—but now there was an edge of ecstasy, of urgency to every thought and joke and touch we shared. We often spoke of how lucky we were, how we'd finally found what mattered. The truth of our relationship was clear, really clear, for the first time, and though we were sorry that it took what it took for to us appreciate what we had . . . well, finally we knew.

We talked and talked. We'd joke our way through each day's appointments—the doctors and nurses loved us—and almost seemed to grow giddier the sicker Jackie became. She had time to think about all the details of her death, including the gravesite in her family's plot. We took an afternoon to visit it—me pushing her chair, with oxygen tank, her father close by. It was her decision, whether to be buried there or not. At first, we were both underwhelmed by the nondescript, suburban style of the cemetery, its stones set flush with the ground, for easier mowing. But when she noticed the heavy-headed catalpa tree almost directly above her plot, a sense of peace came over her, and she smiled. It had always been her favorite kind of tree.

And when, just a few weeks before her death, I was able to tell her that my first poetry book, *The Island*, had been accepted by one of our most distinguished presses, I believe she was even more deeply thrilled than I—clasping my hand, pulling off her oxygen mask to tell me, "Of course." By then we were in each other's skin and felt each other's pain and joy as one.

All that year, we had beaten back dozens of tumors in her brain, her liver, everywhere. But the one that ended her life was the size of a pea, so small it barely showed up on the x-ray. It perforated her lung lining, and wasn't discovered until her lungs were nearly filled with fluid. Once, twice—out of her mind with oxygen deprivation—Jackie's lungs were drained through an outsized needle inserted between her ribs. She said this was the most excruciating procedure of all. But when her lungs began to fill for the third time, she didn't have the strength or will to continue. She said no. The doctor agreed: her lungs were not "viable." We made her comfortable in the master suite of her mother's house, a hospice nurse on duty round the clock, as she drifted into a deep, Ativan-and-morphine-managed coma. The countertops were full of covered dishes; her mother and sister kept busy tending to lavish bouquets left on the porch.

Jackie was only forty-one. She'd lost more than fifty pounds, but still had the heart of a lion. So dying wasn't easy. She was in the deepest sort of coma for nearly two weeks—all her vital functions dramatically suppressed, only three or four reflex breaths per minute—though it seemed unimaginable that she could hang on at all. It's easy to tell when someone's lungs are full: anyone with a stethoscope can hear it. It's a hard thing to say, but when someone you love spends a week or two in a coma without being able to draw air into her lungs, you don't want her to wake up. When all you can hope for is to spare her some pain and terror, that's what you try to do.

A new, elderly hospice nurse showed up one day and introduced herself, projecting confidence and experience as she assumed her place beside the bed and took up her knitting. Within the first hour, I had a talk with her about meds, the timed schedule of supplementary boluses we'd been administering through Jackie's catheter. She riled at this, in what seemed an old-fashioned, common sense way: shaking her head, telling me that at the levels Jackie was receiving, they were unnecessary, she couldn't feel any pain. She declared, "I won't snow a patient." I reminded her that Jackie had been on morphine for over a year, and had built up extraordinary tolerances. "We'll see," was the answer. I bit my lip.

Within a few hours, Jackie's hands, then her entire frame began to tremble, and her temperature crept up to 104. Her pulse, too, began to rise, eventually holding at 120 beats per minute. Jackie's parents, Jack and Neila, seemed inclined to respect the nurse's judgment. I tried to do the same, but kept shooting nervous glances toward her. She merely nodded kindly. These symptoms were normal at "end stage," she said. An hour passed, an anxious, fluttery hour when some of us—Neila and I—might have wondered whether the nurse was right. Then, almost unfathomably, Jackie's right hand rose to her mouth; she seemed to be trying to feel her lips. I moved in quickly beside her, half sitting on the bed, and began dampening her lips with a washcloth. The nurse, in those moments, smiled: she seemed to expect a comeback. Looking up from her knitting, she said, "Well, hello there. How are you?"

Jackie's jaw sawed this way and that, attempting to speak; I kept dampening her parched lips again and again, then her forehead and cheeks. Finally, clearing her throat and gathering herself, she said: "I feel terrible. I really need a shot."

"It's coming, love," I said. "It's on the way." I glared at the nurse, who had roused to action and was already breaking the wrapper of a syringe.

I could see Jackie's eyes moving this way and that beneath her eyelids. Her hand came up to try to clear her eyes of some imagined obstruction. I said, "Wait," and held the washcloth gently but directly on her eyes, for I could see that she was struggling to open them to look at me one last time. But her eyelids were stuck fast and would not open. "Don't worry about it, sweetie, it's okay," I said, as I watched the nurse's thumb push down the plunger. "It's okay, it doesn't make any difference, just relax." Then, on the bed with her, clasping and stroking her hand, I watched as her eyes seemed to calm; at least, they weren't flicking back and forth so much. She held my hand very tightly in her own, and her grip was not the grip of an emaciated, dying woman. It was the grip of the dazzling star I'd seen on the stage at the Kennedy Center; the grip of the woman who believed in me more than I'd ever thought to believe in myself, who'd always taken such joy in my writing, she made me feel—because she felt it herself—it was Christmas when I wrote. Then, knowing that she was slipping under fast, very fast, she pronounced clearly, "I love you."

"I love you, too," I answered, and then, "But you don't have to say it. You don't have to say anything. I know."

What I don't know, and can't imagine, is how she'd done it. Perhaps in the recesses of one last bronchiole, she was still able to take infinitesimal sips of air, or imaginary sips of air; or perhaps in the underworld where she had gone, no oxygen was required. Maybe, I thought, her metabolism was so depressed, that the slightest traces of oxygen and water—absorbed through the skin or nostrils—could suffice for a while. I took it as pure will, though, her soul ceding nothing except on its own terms.

Some might think it was simply pain that woke her. But I didn't think so then, and I don't think so now. She was aware of everything in that room, what we felt and thought, exactly what had been happening. She came back to take her leave—and, satisfied with what she'd found, she let go. There was a slim passageway, just wide enough for her to slip through. I held her hand as a lifetime of minutes slid by, like all those nights in graduate school—looking up in the fullness of all we had, as we'd drift away on the afterglow, the ceiling fan spinning slowly toward oblivion—long after her hand went soft, and I tucked it in at her side again.

At five a.m. on November 18, 1991, her body still trying to do its job—still trying, blindly, to take a breath—she passed.

Jackie had many friends, and hers was an elite, pillar-of-the-community Boone County family, so the funeral was swamped. I met well-wishers by the hundreds, many for the first time. Amidst tearful hugs and condolences, I think I startled some (though of course they were inclined to a charitable view) by often remarking how blessed I was, how our love had come "just in time." And of course I would go through a process of grieving over the next couple of years. But the overwhelming emotion of the moment, of that entire period of my life, was gratitude.

For the warmth, the silken feel, of her hand in my hand—it was still softly burning there. There was a hallowed silence in the townhouse, which I simply wouldn't disturb. For two months I worked in her study, polishing *The Island* for publication. I looked out the window of the study, over the tops of the once-so-lovely hills, where I had wandered as a child—now landscaped, sub-divided, crowned with sodden golf courses. But I always felt her presence: in the next room perhaps, or out on an errand, and I felt the sense of a shared mission, the ongoing work that was neither mine, nor hers, but ours.

Her light step somewhere; her unselfconscious hum somewhere; the ornamental birches brushing the window.

2. Afterward

Still, by spring, I wondered if I should seek some other sort of help. I wasn't sure which world I was living in. Finally deciding it was a spiritual matter, I dialed Sacred Heart Church one afternoon. It couldn't hurt, I thought. I had gone there myself as a child for a couple of years, at my recently divorced mother's somewhat puzzling insistence (no one in my family was Catholic, or had even been baptized). It was still the only church where I'd even remotely felt at home. Sister Margaret answered. I said I was recently widowed and needed to talk with someone. She said, "Yes, of course," asked no questions and, two days later, I walked into the diocese offices behind the church on Walnut Street.

She insisted I call her Maggie, and sat me down in her office cluttered with wire baskets piled with forms and folders, space heater on the floor. "Excuse the mess," she said. "Part of my job is to run the Sunday school." I found a perch on a metal stacking chair. Nothing was as I'd expected: instead of the beatific matron in habit, here was a woman in camel cardigan, braids pinned neatly above her ears.

"Michael, how did you meet your wife?"

And so I told her the story about the cabin in Steamboat Springs, about the plumbing. It was almost like living it all again. I suddenly remembered leaning into the crumbling earthen bank beneath the floor, trying to get a grip on the old iron couplings with a ten-pound pipe wrench clanking in my hands, dirt and sweat in my eyes. The pipes in those cabins always ice-burst in the dead of winter, though I wouldn't discover it until I tried to turn on the water at the beginning of summer. The image of Jackie's face, staring incredulously down at me through a hole in a bathroom floor. "Hullo?" she'd said.

"Oh hi . . . I'll be done in a minute."

Maggie giggled, schoolgirl-style.

"Where did you go for your first date?"

I recalled driving the battered flatbed up the canyon road to Fish Creek Falls—the sense that this lady, this elegant, olive-skinned lady in slacks didn't belong in such a vehicle, in such a place, with such a driver (I spent those summers in straw hat, jeans, torn-off sleeves). But here she was: smiling, her dark eyes shining, smoking a Virginia Slims extravagantly out the passenger window. She was having the time of her life. Standing on the cantilever footbridge at the base of the falls, she marveled at the height of it, the boulder-broken roar of it, cool veil of spray directly in our faces. I kept wondering if being here, being with me was a wrong-side-of-the-tracks thing for her. I recited Bishop's twenty-line poem, "Sandpiper." This was everything, *she* was everything I had never dared to want, and when we kissed in the mist of the falls, we already knew how lucky we were.

"How long before you got married?"

I told her about "living in sin," about the idyllic years in grad school—poetry readings, parties, black box theatre—and tried to summarize year by year. How proud I was of her, the sense of self-containment: all we really needed was each other. Jackie's brilliance, the way she excelled at almost everything. The whole while I talked, I gazed out over the low roofs of Walnut Street, the stark Missouri sky above. It was my life I was looking at, scenes from my childhood mixed in with scenes with Jackie. I tried to explain. When I was thirteen, the six of us—my recently separated mom and all five kids—would ride our bikes, in single file, *here* on Sunday morning . . . three boys in blazers with clip-on ties or dickies, the girls in their summer dresses. A "mother hen with five little chicks," as someone at Mass described it. As reward, on the way home, our mother would buy us all cherry phosphates at Glenview Drug. We were never more a family than on those Sunday mornings. I hadn't stepped foot in Sacred Heart since then.

"I'm starting to wonder about myself," I said.

"Why?" she asked.

"Well, I won't touch Jackie's things. And I hear her in the house. She's with me," I said. "One day, as I was working in the study, I saw a beautiful red fox loping straight toward me, across the golf course, tongue lolling to one side, and I cried out: 'Jackie! Look!'"

"Yes, she is with you," said Maggie.

"Michael," she added, "Nothing we do for each other is in vain. I believe love is eternal." Then she said, "And she'll *always* be with you." And there was no trace of striving in her tone: it was casual, matter-of-fact.

After a moment, she asked about my "spiritual quest"; she mentioned that, besides the school, she ran the RCIA program—the Rite of Christian Initiation for Adults—at Sacred Heart, and invited me to attend an "inquiry session." In case I was curious.

I didn't mind that she asked me this; I could see no reason to mind.

I went to the meetings for a few weeks, and enjoyed them. Two days before my lease ran out, I emptied Jackie's dressers and closets, piled the mink coats in the bed of my truck, and poured the contents of jewelry boxes into a bushel basket. Real pearls, braids of gold and diamonds mixed in with handfuls of the baroque costume jewelry she'd collected for the stage. I drove to the Salvation Army, dumped it all in the center of the concrete floor—much to the astonishment of the volunteers—and walked away. That afternoon, I packed a U-Haul trailer, and before sunrise, I hit the on-ramp back toward Utah.

All that year, it felt like I had the strength of two—almost an unearthly strength. I'd hike back into the desert wilderness for weeks, sometimes. I could draw unemployment in the city without a trace of shame, and did. In springtime, 1992, I finished RCIA at the Newman Center in Salt Lake, was baptized, and found joy in the process. By fall, when the academic year began again, I was back at the University, wrapping up my doctorate. Then the book was out, and I started interviewing for jobs. More importantly, I was free— at least for the time being—free of self-doubts, of second-guessing my personal worth or what I could do for others. And the truth is, Maggie was right; Jackie has always been with me.

3. Sara

I first met Sara in 1991, before Jackie died. I was teaching that fall semester at Westminster College, in Fulton, Missouri. I'd taken the job, a simple sabbatical replacement, because Jackie had urged me to take it. She saw it as a first step toward my profession; she was probably right about that. Her one and only goal in those weeks, as the cancer rapidly overtook her, was to make it to Christmas. She didn't make it to Thanksgiving. Each day, I drove sixty miles to teach my courses in Fulton, and then back to Columbia to take my place at Jackie's side. When Jackie passed, I took only three days off, and then finished out the semester. I felt I needed the human contact, the normalcy.

Sara was a Freshman Composition student of mine that semester. Here is virtually everything I remember of her then. She had gorgeous, liquid-brown eyes. She set up three required conferences with me to discuss her work, but each time, when I took the precious hour or two away from Jackie to meet, Sara didn't show up. This didn't go over well with me, and besides, I'd told the class that I'd count missed conferences as absences. I gave her a B+ for a final grade. I considered the B+ generous; she was very young, after all.

In April 1998, a five-page letter arrived from Sara, addressed to "Professor Mike White, University of North Carolina, Chapel Hill." Somehow, it found me at UNC-Wilmington. I'd nearly forgotten her. She was finishing a master's degree in voice at the University of Missouri, and attending a summer residency at Wake Forest University, in Winston-Salem, North Carolina. On the last page, she wondered if we could meet. And because, that spring, I happened to be passing through Greensboro for a reading in Asheville, we did meet. I had a strangely awkward lunch on that rather prim campus with an anxious and long-limbed beauty. I was confused, but went to my reading, came back on Sunday as I passed through again, and we had another awkward lunch, club sandwiches at a nearby restaurant. I sent a salad back that came with the wrong dressing, and for some reason, this action made Sara seem very anxious. She later told me it made me seem demanding. By the end of that lunch I thought I probably shouldn't see her again. The age difference seemed too pronounced. It was a mistake, I thought.

But when I was dropping her off at her dorm, she suggested we go for a walk by a nearby pond. We ambled into a sheltered grove, and she stopped and turned toward me, smiling. I asked if I could kiss her, and she—amused that I had asked—said yes. I kissed her, passionately but respectfully, and there she showed me such strength of desire I wouldn't have suspected.

On her first visit to Wilmington, we spent a whole weekend on the beach. I sat, half delirious, watching her dash in and out of the jade-green waves in a tiny, black string-bikini. We made out for hours in the moonlit dunes, but didn't yet sleep together. On her second visit, that October, we did—going at it for three straight days and nights, dressing only once, very briefly, to go out for a bite at a nearby Thai restaurant. I can almost excuse myself for marrying her that December. The sex was narcotic. I'd flip over onto my back— heart in my throat, my lungs heaving—and realize that half a day had passed. Also, she was a Missouri girl, a comforting detail that probably carried more weight with me than it ought.

When the lovely little wedding was over, along with the truncated but lovely honeymoon on Bald Head Island, off the coast of Wilmington, and when all the rooms had been repainted and the bride installed, it seemed as if bliss had arrived for good. It seemed as if my lonely childhood, battle with alcoholism, the tragic first marriage, and all the rest of my travails were well behind me now. Karma and perseverance had finally paid off.

I'd gotten tenure, and was teaching, writing, getting back to my normal work. My material life was organized for the first (and last) time: towels neatly stacked away, socks matched, hedges cut off at their knees. Sara was an outgoing hit with everyone, was gardening enthusiastically, and had begun working part-time jobs. She was even starting to get along with my dog, a hyper black lab named Elizabeth. And if there was still more lust than love, that was fine for now.

The odd thing is, although my first marriage taught me everything I knew about love, and would seem therefore to have prepared me for my second marriage, in fact it did the opposite. I was far too confident with Sara, partly because I'd built up my confidence sky-high with Jackie.

Everything I wrote, for many years, I wrote for Jackie. I'd stay up all night drafting a poem, and leave a clean copy out on the kitchen table when I turned in at dawn, and it would thrill Jackie to the bone when she read it over her morning coffee. My knowing that a poem I wrote could do that for her kept me going. Not only my poetry, but almost everything else about me—my jokes, my wanderlust, even my crooked and dented nose—delighted Jackie. She fell in love with the idea of the A. A. fellowship (although she wasn't an alcoholic), and enjoyed going to open meetings at my home group in Salt Lake City every week. She found them comforting. And in the last few years, no matter what Jackie and I went through—surgery after surgery, grief and rage and madness with no end in sight—we kept discovering that, together, we were able to face it. Never had I imagined I could matter so much to another human being.

In my first year with Sara, everyone I knew could hardly believe how I'd lucked out, with such a vivacious, multi-talented beauty. I could hardly believe it myself. She seemed equally thrilled and amused with me. But as time went on, it turned out that life with a poet wasn't the passionate, expressive lark she'd expected—she hadn't counted on the hours of quiet I required. Within a year, she'd begun to act resentful. When she attended a large open meeting at my A. A. home group in Wilmington, there was something about the typically riotous and motley crew that she found disturbing; she never went back. She wanted me to get my nose fixed. I finally said, what the hell, I would (but never did). My snoring bothered her, and she often woke me to make me stop.

In this depressing course of events, the bright spot was Sophia's birth and the months that followed, the incredible fact of an inexpressibly perfect blonde baby clinging to my arm like a spider monkey wherever I went. But just after Sophia's first birthday, things began unraveling again.

One night, hoping to make a turnaround, I had a surprise for Sara. I'd written a poem that celebrated our marriage, and it had just been published in an excellent university journal. I presented it to her as we lay side by side in bed. She gave it a glance, shrugged, then lay the magazine down on the bed between us and took up her novel again. I felt half my resolve die in that moment. Later that year, she said she didn't like the way I smelled. I started sleeping on the sofa. One day, I stood at the front door looking out and wondering what had happened.

An Ending

[*May*]

1. Tracery

Twenty minutes after taking off from Gatwick, I raise the shade and look out over the branching currents of the North Atlantic Drift, all glittering like silver tracery. Most of us have already adjusted the volume, settled into the movie or sports-page or paperback. Five miles above the Arctic ice, a sense of peace presides. As I peer down through the little window beside me, I begin to make out individual icebergs, schools of far-flung, glinting floes—punctuated by their shadows, thrown onto the mirror-green sea beside them.

The squeal of a young girl behind me makes me smile—thinking of Sophia. My little presents are safely packed, waiting for our reunion. I wonder what I will say to her, I wonder who I am to her. I'm The Green Dragon Club. I'm summers sitting beside the YWCA pool, watching her flip and dolphin-kick. Each time she comes up for air, I'm there.

The flight attendant asks if I'd like a snack.

Who is she? I wonder, smiling out of her cloud. Yes, of course I would.

For another minute now, I imagine that sweet passivity of poolside / rinkside / music lesson / playground, the state of being a parent. Lying on a lounge near the shallow end of the pool, some novel facedown on my chest, I love to stare for hours at patches of sky through pines. My hearing tuned to distinguish playful cries from pain, from fear—and otherwise adrift.

Up here, I'm holding Gowing's book in my lap—as I have so often over the past year or so. I like to keep it close to me, but frankly I don't often open it anymore. All my earnest reading, the visit with Kees Kaldenbach—all that urgent wandering, intent on figuring

out Vermeer's hold on me after the first day in the Rijksmuseum—
much of that seems distant and a little amusing to me now. It's like
how we respond to the loss of love—with Match.com and counseling and all the rest. The problem is that the object of love isn't really
the issue. What's missing is a verb, not a noun. You can look into
these faces from three hundred and forty years ago, and feel it.

At ease in my mind, this book in my lap, the map of the world
in silver fishscale tracery beneath me: here is the end of obsession.

2. A Solution

When Sophia was still an infant, I remember the inexhaust-
ible wonder in her gaze. She'd stare so seekingly into my eyes for
hours—first one eye, then the other eye, and then doze off before
beginning again . . . In those first months, the child is on a mission,
it seems, to memorize the face of love. How astonishing to see and
be seen, to be truly seen for the first time.

What could equal it? There are moments when the terms of
one's own life are irrevocably changed by simply looking into a
lover's eye, when crazed with love or parting or sorrow—a handful of times, if we're lucky. In such times, I have felt the weight of
all I might say, all I might have said—the impossibility of articu-
lating anything out of the crushing welter of emotion—but also
the mercy of being released from such a burden because, just then,
with nothing between you and the one you love, you both already
know. As I told Jackie in her last seconds of consciousness: "you
don't have to say anything. I know." Or even when looking into
Sara's eyes through the little window: *I know.*

What if a painter painted virtually nothing but such moments?
What if he held his immense gifts in reserve, solely for such states of
recognition? This is what Vermeer did. In the event of our arrival—
that moment when, occupied with their music lesson or holding a
glass of wine—his women turn and look and almost exclaim, "It's
you."

It was Arthur Wheelock who called this "the momentary

interruption"—the glance out toward the viewer just before the girl returns to her suitor. As if one backward glance, one touch, can reach through a person's entire life. As if, when Eurydice turns, we are there. But almost every Vermeer, every attempt at illumination contains some "momentary interruption" of time—whether anyone looks out at us or not—encoded into the sheen of surfaces that flood the senses and fill the mind with rapture.

My restoration is in that instant. As William Blake wrote: "If the doors of perception were cleansed every thing would appear to man as it is, infinite. / For man has closed himself up, till he sees all things thro' narow chinks of his cavern." This is true for me; the struggle is to see.

What I've experienced in Vermeer isn't quite like the recovery of A. A.—the kind you have to work for—because Vermeer has done most of the work himself, his visions so clear they "cleanse" our human sight. He aspires not simply to paint for a viewer like myself, but also to *become* me—to stand where I stand, feel what I feel, dream what I dream looking into the looking glass. In this way, his self-effacing, chameleon-like power seems an example of what Keats calls man's "negative capability": " . . . when man is capable of being in uncertainties, Mysteries, doubts without any irritable reaching after fact & reason."

The painting stares at us, more powerfully charged the longer we meet its gaze. But the meaning, of course, is inside us; part of the painting's power is its effortless access. There's a sense of space to begin with; and the painting speaks of things, the touch of things, with an optical as well as a lyrical authority. It grants the world its due: "our clouds, our sky."

No small part of the poignancy of *The Girl with a Pearl Earring* or *Girl with a Red Hat*, for instance, is a result of this urgency, this flash of emotion—seen and felt instantaneously. The painting meets us there—where we are most aware and most ourselves, certain of nothing except that everything is changed. But even the paintings that don't stare out at us—*The Milkmaid* or *Woman Holding a Balance,* for instance—work in a similar way. We still find ourselves confronted with an extraordinarily intimate image, a reflection, with effortless access to our private selves—so that what she feels, we feel the instant we look at her. It's unsettling to remain unacknowledged, even as we stand in the room with her; we hold our breath reflexively, so as not to disturb her. She is the center of this world—the lustrous pearls or bread-crusts incandescing beneath her touch—and by the time she looks around, we'll be gone.

3. Spring

Because this is Swiss Air, the in-flight snack isn't pretzels. I peel off the plastic film covering the tray: there's a small tin of pâté, a wedge of ripe brie, cut fruit in a plastic cup, water crackers, also a biscuit, a pat of foil-wrapped Normandy butter; a dense bar of Swiss chocolate, a cup of chocolate mousse for dessert. Sun slants in from the left.

Five miles up in the brilliant blue, I'm on my way to see Sophia, riding a wave of gratitude that I can't get to the bottom of. There are troughs of turbulence above Iceland and Greenland, jostling and upsetting the drowsy passengers. I have no desire to sleep, to read, to watch the movie, no desire to do anything beyond unwrapping a round of Brie and a water biscuit. I'm soaring in complete contentment over the uninhabitable north. It's mid-May, it's almost June—then summer, and my blessed, uninterrupted four weeks with my daughter, and all the blackberries we can pick.

4. Her Face

I reach for the cup of mousse in its recessed corner of the tray. The image on the peel-off foil lid suddenly catches my eye. Although the two colors—blue and yellow—are exaggerated and garish, it is still "Milkmaid;" she is a popular brand of mousse! "La Laitiére," it seems, is not only the French translation of the painting's title, but a Nestle Suisse line of chilled desserts, including the "Secret de Mousse" I am holding.

She appears on the top as a bust, about two-thirds of an inch in height. Her face is so small that none of its nuances are conveyed. Not surprisingly, the pitcher and the bowl into which she pours are much too big. There is no room about her, no table, no still-life—only the woman, the pitcher, and the bowl against the yellow and white ground of the logo . . . Vermeer's color scheme, his maid, gaudily reincarnated as product image.

I remove the lid and place it at the side of the tray. The mousse itself is about what I'd expect: dissolves like sea foam on the tongue. When I'm finished, I carefully clean the inside of the lid with a white paper napkin. I fold it in half, wrap it in the cellophane the napkin came in, and pocket it safely in my denim shirt. I won't look at it again until I write the last page of this manuscript.

It's simply a keepsake, here at the end of my travels. But it feels like a sign, a note of grace—this face that called from across the room, delivered into my hands at the end.

I close the shade against the glare of Greenland beneath. Then I close my eyes. Drifting off, I pat the wrapper safe in my pocket.

Not to make too much of it. Such sentimentality, I think.

Reason says: just a random occurrence. Reason says: just one of those things.

But not this time. Not for me. I know a gift when I see it.

SUGGESTED READING

Bailey, Anthony. *A Web of Social History* (Princeton University Press, 1989).

Bailey, Anthony. *Vermeer: A View of Delft* (Henry Holt and Company, 2001).

Gowing, Lawrence. *Vermeer* (University of California Press, 1955).

Liedtke, Walter. *A View of Delft: Vermeer and his Contemporaries* (Yale University Press, 2001)

Liedtke, Walter. *Vermeer: The Complete Paintings* (Abrams, 2008).

Montias, John. *Vermeer and His Milieu* (Princeton University Press, 1991).

Snow, Edward. *A Study of Vermeer* (University of California Press, 1994).

Steadman, Philip. *Vermeer's Camera: Uncovering the Truth Behind the Masterpieces* (Oxford University Press, 2001).

Wheelock, Arthur. *Vermeer: The Complete Works* (Abrams, 1997).

ACKNOWLEDGMENTS

Two books on Vermeer were ideal traveling companions. Lawrence Gowing's classic *Vermeer* is the first book of art criticism I've ever devoured as avidly as a mystery and as obsessively as poetry. Edward Snow's ravishing *A Study of Vermeer* helped map out the subterranean threads that run through Vermeer's oeuvre.

Dr. Kees Kaldenbach's command of art and history continues to shape my thinking on Vermeer in unexpected and gracious ways.

Jonathan Janson, a central figure in contemporary Vermeer studies, has helped me immeasurably. As a working painter, Janson writes with intimacy and authority about Vermeer and about the art of painting in general. His website, *The Essential Vermeer*, is one of the great art troves of the internet, visited daily not only by experts in the field, but also by countless students, travelers, and amateur Vermeer lovers like myself.

Brooke Hopkins, a beloved former professor of mine at the University of Utah, read and wisely reflected on these pages as they were first written. Brooke continued to guide my project even after a bike accident in 2008 left him paralyzed. He passed away on July 31, 2013.

I also received generous critiques from Bob Reiss, Dana Sachs, and Sarah Messer. Thanks to each from the bottom of my heart, and to all my friends at the University of North Carolina at Wilmington. Love to Bekki and Wendy and Clyde and Peter and especially to my daughter, Sophia.

I'm grateful to the Ucross Foundation, in Ucross, Wyoming; to the Djerassi Foundation, in Woodale, California; and to the Anderson Center, in Red Wing, Minnesota, for blissful residencies where I wrote this book.

The last debt is perhaps the greatest: to Karen Braziller, whose tireless and masterful editing polished each of these sentences over and over again.

ABOUT THE AUTHOR

MICHAEL WHITE is Professor of Creative Writing at The University of North Carolina at Wilmington. He was educated at the University of Missouri and the University of Utah, where he received his doctorate in English and Creative Writing. His poetry collections are *The Island, Palma Cathedral* (winner of the Colorado Prize), *Re-entry* (winner of the Vassar Miller Prize), and *Vermeer in Hell* (winner of the Lexi Rudnitsky Editor's Choice Award). His poems and essays have appeared in *The Paris Review, The New Republic, The Kenyon Review, The Best American Poetry,* and many other magazines and anthologies.